BookCaps™ Presents:

The Importance of Being Earnest
In Plain and Simple English

Oscar Wilde

Includes Study Guide, Complete Unabridged Book, Historical Context, Biography and Character Index

BookCaps™ Study Guides
www.bookcaps.com

Cover Image © LiliGraphie - Fotolia.com

Table of Contents

Study Guide: The Importance of Being Earnest

Historical Context

During the late 1800's, the British Empire was at its height. The English aristocracy was far above the lower classes and was seen as rich and snobbish to everyone but themselves. Because of this gap between the classes, there was a lot of social unrest, and many authors during this period wrote novels and plays dealing with social issues. Marriage plots and social comedies were still popular among the higher class, and The Importance of Being Earnest combines the traditional marriage plot with a witty exploration of Victorian social issues.

The Importance of Being Earnest was written by Oscar Wilde and premiered in London in February of 1895. Oscar Wilde was born in Dublin, Ireland, in 1854, but settled in London after going to school there. Because of his intellect, his outrageous style of dress and his poems, novel, and plays, Wilde became a part of English high society, moving around in fashionable intellectual circles. By the 1890's, Oscar Wilde was one of the most popular playwrights in London, and The Importance of Being Earnest is known today as his crowning achievement. It was, however, his last play, as a series of incidents after the opening took Wilde to court, where he was revealed to be having an affair with another man.

When this information came to light, themes in the play such as dual identities and hints of the homosexual culture of London suddenly became scandalous, and the play was subsequently cancelled. Oscar Wilde was sent to prison, where he continued writing poems, but after his release ended up broke and on the streets. He never released another play.

The Importance of Being Earnest has many hints of Oscar Wilde's autobiography and unique (at the time) view of high society. Characters such as Algernon, for instance, were known as Dandy's. They were young men overly concerned with appearances and dress, and in all of Wilde's plays, engaged in circular philosophical conversations. Wilde supposedly modeled these characters after himself, as he was known for his love of dress and conversation. In The Importance of Being Earnest, Algernon reveals the serious and trivial backwardness of Victorian high society through his witticisms, which infuriate more sensible characters, such as Jack.

The parallel between Jack and Algernon's "Bunburying", or assumption of double identities for the purpose of going into the town and country, relates strongly to Wilde's own double life as a homosexual. In London high society, this theme resonated strongly with many who adopted new identities for the sole purpose of having affairs or visiting the brothels without risking their position in society and/or their marriage.

Although The Importance of Being Earnest presents itself as a trivial comedy, the themes it explores are anything but trivial. Wilde's backwards presentation of seriousness, manners and marriage still resonate with audiences today.

Plot Summary

The play opens at Algernon Moncrieff's flat in London. Algernon's Aunt Augusta (Lady Bracknell) and cousin Gwendolyn Fairfax are coming to visit, and Lane is preparing tea for them. Jack Worthing, a friend of Algernon's, arrives before the women do, announcing himself as "Ernest". Algernon finds this curious, since he found a cigarette case inscribed to an "Uncle Jack" from "little Cecily". Jack admits that he goes by Ernest in town and Jack in the country. "Little Cecily" is his young ward and believes Ernest to be Jack's older brother.

Algernon reveals that he, too, uses a made-up persona to escape from unwanted social situations. Algernon's is called Bunbury and is his invalid friend constantly on the edge of death. Using Bunbury as an excuse is called "Bunburying" and Algernon says Jack is an expert at it, with his "brother" Ernest. Jack protests that he isn't, and intends to get rid of Ernest as soon as he's married Gwendolyn, whom he plans to propose to today.

Lady Bracknell and Gwendolyn arrive, and Algernon uses Bunbury as an excuse not to go to his Aunt's dinner party. He distracts Lady Bracknell, giving Jack and Gwendolyn a chance to talk privately. Jack proposes, and Gwendolyn accepts, saying that it has always been her dream to marry a man named Ernest. Lady Bracknell comes back in and reproaches the two of them, telling Gwendolyn to leave. She questions Jack's intentions and his heritage to see if he is a suitable match for her daughter, but after finding out that Jack was found in a handbag at a railway station and has no parents, she declares that he will never marry Gwendolyn.

She leaves, and Gwendolyn comes back in. She asks for Jack's address in the country, so she can send him mail, and Algernon, eavesdropping, writes the address down. When everyone is gone, Algernon plans on taking a "bunbury" trip to Jack's estate to meet Cecily.

At Jack's manor, Cecily and her governess Miss Prism are in the garden. The Chasuble comes by, and Miss Prism takes a walk with him, flirting boldly. When the governess is gone, Merriman, the servant, announces the arrival of Ernest Worthing, and Algernon introduces himself to Cecily. He finds that he has finally met his match, as Cecily is as witty as he. Algernon falls in love with her and plans to stay until Monday, when Jack is scheduled to return.

Jack, however, returns early, dressed in mourning clothes, announcing the death of his wicked brother Ernest and asking the Chasuble if he can be christened. Cecily tells Jack that Ernest is inside and brings Algernon out. Jack is outraged at Algernon's deceit but doesn't reveal the truth. When Jack is gone, Algernon proposes to Cecily, for he has fallen for her beauty and wit. Cecily accepts because she has always wanted to marry a man named Ernest, and Algernon exits the stage, also to ask the Chasuble about his christening.

With the two men gone chasing the Chasuble, Cecily sits alone in the garden. Merriman announces the arrival of Gwendolyn Fairfax, and the two women sit down to tea. They soon begin arguing, since they both believe they are engaged to Ernest. The men return and their real identities are revealed. The women, scorned, go into the house.

Algernon and Jack argue in the garden, eating muffins, and Jack tries to get Algernon to leave. When he won't, the two decide to go into the house to confront the women. Cecily and Gwendolyn soon forgive them since they both have plans to be christened under the name "Ernest".

Lady Bracknell enters; she has followed Gwendolyn. She declares that neither couple will be married, but changes her mind when she discovers Cecily is heir to a small fortune. Jack tries to strike a deal with Lady Bracknell, saying he will give Cecily permission to marry if she gives Gwendolyn permission.

The Chasuble enters, followed by Miss Prism. Lady Bracknell demands Miss Prism tell her what happened to the baby. Twenty-eight years ago Miss Prism misplaced Algernon's older brother, leaving him in a handbag. Jack retrieves the bag and is revealed to be Ernest John Moncrieff. There is rejoicing, as all the couples can now be engaged.

Themes

Double Identities

Both the main male characters in the play, Algernon and Jack, use double identities to have more freedom moving around in society. Jack uses his made-up brother, Ernest, as his name in town, and as an excuse to come to town more often. Algernon uses his made-up friend, Bunbury, an invalid who is constantly ill, as an excuse to get out of unwanted arrangements. He calls this habit "Bunburying", and believes every man should have a double identity. By the end of the play, however, when everyone is engaged, both Bunbury and Ernest are no longer needed.

Disconnect to the Past

All of the young characters have unusually vague or nonexistent pasts. Algernon can't remember his parents, Jack was found in a handbag at a railway station, Gwendolyn knows her mother but never mentions her past, and Cecily writes in her diary for fear of forgetting her memories. The past is nothing more than a way to get one's wishes in the present. For Jack, this is getting engaged to Gwendolyn. He sees no reason why he shouldn't be allowed to marry her, but Gwendolyn's mother insists her daughter cannot marry someone with no parents. When this mystery is solved, Jack doesn't even ask for more details about his parents.

The Importance of Appearances

The characters in the play are all overly concerned with appearances, some more than others. Algernon, especially, is famous for always being over-dressed, and cannot help but comment on everyone's clothing, and choice of snack served at tea. When Lady Bracknell discovers Algernon's engagement to Cecily, she examines the girl's appearance from head to toe and announces that her profile has "social promise". When Jack shows up in mourning clothes, both Algernon and Cecily tell him to change immediately because he looks ridiculous.

Manners

Much like the character's preoccupation with appearances and beauty, manners also play a significant role in the way the play unfolds. Every decision is made on the base of whether or not it is appropriate. Jack, for instance, accuses Algernon of not acting like a gentleman by coming to the manor under the pretense of being Jack's brother, and accuses Algernon of treating Cecily "inappropriately". Lady Bracknell is the character most concerned with proper manners and is constantly obsessing about what other members of society will say if someone acts out of line.

Institution of Marriage

Since The Importance of Being Earnest is, at heart, a marriage plot (the play ends with three engagements) there is much discussion about the institution of marriage. At the beginning of the play when Jack wants to propose to Gwendolyn, Algernon advises against it, pointing out the horrors of marriage. Lady Bracknell, after visiting one of her recently widowed friends, and declares that she looks twenty years younger. Since marriages were often made for social status rather than love, they weren't known to be positive. However, Algernon falls in love with Cecily and throws all his previous advice about marriage away when he proposes.

Seriousness and Triviality

Throughout the play, there is a constant switch between seriousness and triviality. Algernon declares all serious matters trivial and all trivial matters serious. This theme continues in the character's dialogue and treatment of matters. Algernon, for instance, when a serious event occurs (the women find out the men's deceit) he concerns himself with a truly trivial matter (the muffins being served at tea). The play itself is a twist on this; although it is a comedy filled with triviality, it proves itself to have a much more serious nature.

Philosophy and Witticisms

The dialogue of The Importance of Being Earnest is filled with constant witticisms and circular conversation, so relentless it is, at times, hard to follow. Every character engages in this type of philosophical conversation, some more than others. Algernon and Cecily are especially philosophical, and Algernon is modeled after Oscar Wilde himself, who was a fan of fast-paced conversation. Even sensible characters, such as Lady Bracknell, constantly turn the conversation around to their political or ideological philosophies.

Satire

The Importance of Being Earnest, though a marriage plot by structure, is part comedy, part satire of Victorian high society. Wilde places such an emphasis on triviality, appearances, and manners that the play inevitably becomes a comedy, for there is no other way to take it. Wilde exposes the aspects of high society that he dislikes, even though he is trapped in that very world. It is the satire of society that makes this play so relevant, even in our present day.

Artificiality

The world of the play is so artificially constructed, it cannot be reality. This allowed Wilde to use the play satirically without angering anyone. Since the characters and dialogue are so fake, they could make a serious point without actually being taken seriously. This artificiality reveals itself in the simple-mindedness of the characters, the relentlessly witty dialogue, and the convenience with which the problems of the play are solved. Much like a modern day sitcom, aspects of the characters and places are believable, but they are taken to the extreme for comedic effect.

Comedic Farce

Throughout the play, Wilde uses elements of traditional comedic farce to move the plot along. Unfortunate timing, such as Gwendolyn visiting Cecily right when Algernon and Jack leave, allow for hilarious misunderstandings to take place. The confusion of identities is a classic farcical move, used to create irony. Much of the play is funny because the audience knows information that certain characters don't, and, therefore, are in on the joke. The misunderstandings are all cleared up at the end, allowing for the marriage plot to come to a conclusion.

Characters

Algernon Moncrieff ("Algy")

A young, eligible bachelor who lives in a fashionable flat in West London. An embodiment of the "Dandy" stereotypes often present in Wilde's work, Algernon is witty, overly concerned with his appearance, and tries hard to be pessimistic and never take anything seriously. Algernon despises the institution of marriage until he meets Cecily, who he falls in love with for her ability to challenge him in conversation.

Jack Worthing (Uncle Jack, John)

Jack Worthing is Algernon's friend. In town, he goes by the name of Ernest, but, at his country home, he is known as Jack. He is in love with Gwendolyn and is highly optimistic and romantic, in direct contrast to Algernon. One of the more sensible characters, he constantly reprimands Algernon for being heartless and ungentlemanly. As a baby, he was found in a handbag and doesn't know who his true parents are. In an unlikely turn of events, he finds out that he is actually Algy's older brother and real name is Ernest.

Lady Bracknell (Aunt Augusta)

The voice of appropriateness in the play, Lady Bracknell is Gwendolyn's mother and Algernon's Aunt. Her only concerns are social status and fortune, and she represents the shallowness of Victorian high society. She constantly objects to the engagements in the play, and the couples must receive her consent before they can marry.

Gwendolyn Fairfax

Gwendolyn is in love with Jack Worthing, though she knows him by the name of Ernest Worthing. She accepts his proposal, saying that she has always wanted to marry a man named Ernest and that she wouldn't accept a man with any other name. She is beautiful, intelligent and cultivated, though, like many of the characters, shallow. She find's Jack's mysterious origins intriguing, but refuses to marry him if his name is Jack.

Cecily Cardew

The grand-daughter of Thomas Cardew, the man who raised Jack Worthing, she grew up as Jack's ward. Eighteen and mischievous, she is quick witted, although she hates studying. She falls in love with Ernest from Jack's stories of him and writes about their courtship in her diary. Her companion is her governess, Miss Prism. Like Gwendolyn, she dreamed of marrying a man named Ernest, and she accepts Algernon's proposal under his false name.

Miss Prism

Cecily's governess of three years, Miss Prism is a respectable, intellectual woman. It becomes apparent that she is in love with Doctor Chasuble and spends time with him whenever possible. As a younger woman, Miss Prism worked for Lord Bracknell and accidentally misplaced their baby in her handbag. The baby turned out to be Jack Worthing.

Dr. Chasuble

The local priest, Dr. Chasuble often visits Mr. Worthing's manner because he enjoys Miss Prism's company. Although he takes walks with her, and flirts with her, because of his priesthood he is required to be celibate. When Algernon and Jack want to change their names, they go to Dr. Chasuble to be christened.

Bunbury

Algernon's made up invalid friend. Bunbury is constantly sick, verging on the edge of death, which allows Algernon to avoid any engagements he finds uninteresting. Algernon calls this avoidance "Bunburying" and develops a culture with rules and philosophies around the practice.

Ernest

Jack's imaginary brother, Ernest Worthing. Jack uses the name Ernest in town, and when he gets back to the country he tells Miss Prism and Cecily his exploits under his double identity. Because of these exploits, Cecily becomes interested in Ernest and falls in love with him.

Lane

Algernon's manservant at his flat in London. Lane prepares the tea, announces guests, and cleans up after Algernon. Lane and Algernon engage in playful banter, and Lane is familiar with his master's philosophies, expressing them himself. It is not clear if his manner is serious or sarcastic during his arguments with Algernon.

Merriman

The manservant at Jack Worthing's country manor. Merriman doesn't have much interaction with the characters, except to announce their entrance and perform small tasks such as serving tea.

Play Summary

Act I

The scene opens on Algernon Moncrieff's flat in Half-Moon Street. In the luxurious morning room, Lane, Algernon's manservant, is setting the tea. In the background, there is a piano playing. The piano stops, and Algernon walks into the room. He asks Lane about his playing, and Lane, in an attempt to prevent offense, says that it isn't polite to listen to other people playing. Algernon admits that his playing isn't good, but defends himself by saying that he plays with true emotion.

Algernon then asks Lane if the cucumber sandwiches for Lady Bracknell and Gwendolyn are ready. The Lady Bracknell is Algernon's aunt, and Gwendolyn his cousin. The two women are coming over to his flat for tea-time today, and he wants everything ready.

When the cucumber sandwiches are placed on the table, Algernon promptly begins eating them. He converses with Lane about the fact that every time he invites bachelors over, they drink all his champagne. Lane thinks it is because married hosts never keep good champagne in the house, and Algernon shudders at the thought of marriage.

Lane thinks marriage isn't so miserable and admits having married once on a misunderstanding before leaving the room to get more tea. Algernon talks to himself about the importance of the lower classes to provide a convincing example for the rest, and how Lane fails in this regard. He thinks the lower class as a whole has no sense of moral responsibility.

When Lane comes back, he introduces a guest, Ernest Worthing, otherwise known as Jack. Algernon asks if he is in town for business or pleasure, and Jack says pleasure. The two of them immediately begin a bantering conversation, and Algernon asks why he hasn't seen Jack in a while.

Jack has been in the countryside, and professes it was boring. The only people around were his neighbors, and he thinks they are horrid people. Jack wonders why Algernon is serving cucumber sandwiches, and Algernon admits that his aunt, Lady Bracknell, and Gwendolyn are coming over for tea.

Algernon says his aunt won't be happy to see Jack back, as she disapproves of his incessant flirting with Gwendolyn. There is more banter, and Algernon says the only thing worse than Jack flirting with Gwendolyn, is how Gwendolyn constantly flirts back.

Jack admits that he is madly in love with Gwendolyn and that he came back in town for the sole purpose of proposing to her.

Algernon gives his witty reply, which is he thought Jack came to town for pleasure and not business. Jack doesn't understand why proposing to the one he loves can't be pleasurable. Algernon admits that it is romantic to be in love and to flirt with women, but he believes it is unromantic to propose. After the proposal, all the excitement is over because then the two have a business arrangement.

During this conversation, Jack reaches over to take a cucumber sandwich, and Jack slaps his hand away, saying they are for his aunt and Gwendolyn. Algernon has been eating the sandwiches throughout the whole scene, so this is done purely to annoy Jack. Algernon takes some bread and butter out from under the table, saying Jack can help himself to the platter, as he ordered it for Gwendolyn.

Jack eats the bread and butter so enthusiastically; Algernon accuses him of acting as if he and Gwendolyn are already engaged. He then goes on to say that Jack and Gwendolyn most likely will not be married, because they would need Algernon's approval, and Algernon doesn't want to give his consent. Jack is confused, until it is revealed that Gwendolyn is Algernon's first cousin.

When Jack asks why Algernon should not give his consent, Algernon asks him who Cecily is. Jack says the name doesn't sound familiar, and Algernon rings the bell for Lane and asks him to bring Jack's cigarette case. When Algernon has the case, he opens it and begins to read the inscription on the inside, which reveals the case is a present from "little Cecily" with "fondest love".

Jack accuses Algernon of being ungentlemanly, but Algernon insists he must know who Cecily is. Jack tells Algernon that Cecily is his aunt and follows Algernon around the room trying to get the cigarette case back.

Algernon questions Jack's story, asking why, in the inscription, Cecily calls Jack "Uncle Jack". If Jack is Cecily's nephew, why would she call Jack uncle? In addition, Algernon points out that Jack's name is actually Ernest.

Jack protests insisting that his name is Jack. Algernon argues, saying his name is Ernest, and it fits because Jack is the most earnest person Algernon knows. He takes one of Jack's business cards with the name Ernest Worthing on it, keeping it as proof. Jack says in town he is known as Ernest but in the country he is known as Jack, and that he got the cigarette case in the country.

Jack agrees to tell Algernon the story of Cecily, if he gives the case back. Algernon does so, and they sit down on the couches.

Thomas Cardew, the man who adopted Jack as a child, made him guardian of his grand-daughter, Cecily Cardew, after his death. Cecily calls Jack uncle out of respect and lives at Jack's estate in the country under the tutor of Miss Prim, her governess.

Algernon says that still doesn't explain why Jack has two different names. Jack admits he invented a younger brother Ernest who lived in the city, and Algernon accuses Jack of being an advanced Bunburyist. Jack demands to know the meaning of that statement. Algernon has invented an alter-ego as well, named Bunbury, whose constant sickness allows him to skip unpleasant engagements.

While they are on the subject of unpleasant engagements, Algernon asks Jack if he can join him for dinner instead of dining with his Aunt Augusta. Jack thinks he better dine with his family, but Algernon insists that his Aunt always sits him next to married women who flirt with their husbands. He believes that is inappropriate behavior, and would rather dine with Jack where he can have some pleasant company.

Algernon also says that he better explain the rules of Bunburying to Jack, but Jack insists he is going to kill Ernest. If he marries Gwendolyn, he will have no need for Ernest. Algernon disagrees, saying that if Jack marries he will have even more need of Ernest than before. Jack tells Algernon not to be so cynical.

The bell rings, and Algernon says his Aunt Augusta and Gwendolyn must be here. Algernon agrees to distract his aunt, so Jack has a chance to propose to Gwendolyn, if Jack invites him to dinner. Jack thanks Algernon and Lane enters the room, announcing Lady Bracknell and Mrs. Fairfax.

Lady Bracknell greets Algernon with a smile and gives Jack a cold bow. Jack pays his compliments to Gwendolyn, and the two sit down together in the corner of the room.

Aunt Augusta apologizes to Algernon for being late, saying that she had to pay a visit to her friend Lady Harbury, whose husband just passed away. She professes she has never seen a woman so transformed, and that Lady Harbury already looks twenty years younger. Algernon agrees as he has heard her transformation has been quite profound.

Aunt Augusta asks Algernon for some cucumber sandwiches, and Algernon goes over to the plate, expressing shock that it is empty. He asks Lane why there are no cucumber sandwiches, and Lane covers Algernon's tracks by saying there were no cucumbers at the market. Algernon apologizes to his aunt, who asks Gwendolyn to come sit next to her. Gwendolyn tells Aunt Augusta that she is acceptable where she is, and Algernon and his aunt resume conversing.

Aunt Augusta says that she is looking forward to dinner, and Algernon tells her his dear friend Bunbury is ill again and that he won't be able to make the engagement. Aunt Augusta remarks that Bunbury has curiously poor health and says it is unhealthy for Algernon to constantly be around someone so sick. Young people should concern themselves with health and not sickness. She still wants to make sure Algernon will come to her party on Saturday, and Algernon agrees that he will. In order to distract her, Algernon asks her to listen to a piece of music he's come up with and leads her to the music room, leaving Gwendolyn and Jack alone.

Jack tries to engage in small talk, but Gwendolyn wishes he wouldn't, saying it always feels like small talk actually means something else. Jack tells her that this time she is right, and expresses his admiration for Gwendolyn, who responds in kind. Jack is surprised and delighted, and Gwendolyn goes on to say that she always believed it was her destiny to marry a man named Ernest because it is the perfect name.

Jack asks her if she would still love him if his name was something else, perhaps Jack. Gwendolyn says she could never love a man named Jack, as all the Jacks she knows are horrid and dull. Jack realizes he must change his name immediately, so the two can get married.

Gwendolyn tells Jack that if he is going to propose, that she will accept his offer. He gets down on one knee and begins making his proposal. She makes fun of him, saying that he hasn't had much practice proposing to women. Jack says that is because Gwendolyn is the only woman he's ever loved.

At this point, Lady Bracknell enters the room, and commands Jack to get up. Gwendolyn retorts to her mother that Jack isn't finished and that they are engaged. Lady Bracknell is angry and tells Gwendolyn to go wait in the car. She tells her daughter sternly that any marriage she enters into will be arranged by her parents and that she cannot choose who she marries. On her way out, Jack and Gwendolyn blow kisses to each other behind Lady Bracknell's back. Gwendolyn finally leaves, and Lady Bracknell turns to Jack.

She requests him to sit, because she has a few questions she needs to ask him. Jack says that he prefers to stand, and Lady Bracknell says it is all the same to her before pulling out a pen and paper.

She has a list of appropriate suitors for Gwendolyn, which Jack is not on. If he answers her questions to her satisfaction, then he might be able to get on that list.

Lady Bracknell asks Jack if he smokes. Jack says yes, and Lady Bracknell approves, saying all men should have a past-time. She asks how old he is, to which Jack replies twenty-nine. Lady Bracknell believes that a good age to be married. She asks Jack if he believes he knows everything or nothing, and Jack says he knows nothing. Jack makes seven or eight thousand a year in investments, which Lady Bracknell approves of. She also seems happy that he has a country estate. She tells Jack, however, that Gwendolyn cannot only reside in the country, and asks if he has a town house. Jack does, but it is lent to an elderly Lady in an "unfashionable" part of town.

Lady Bracknell moves on to what she calls "minor matters", and asks about his politics and parents. Jack doesn't concern himself much with politics and doesn't have either of his parents. Lady Bracknell seems interested in this and wants to know what happened for him to lose two parents. She says that to lose one parent is a misfortune, but to lose two seems like carelessness.

Jack admits to Lady Bracknell that his parents didn't die, that, in fact, he doesn't know who his parents are. Lady Bracknell is astounded, and demands to know details. Jack tells her that he was found as a baby by Thomas Cardew. She asks where, and he reveals that Mr. Cardew found him in a handbag at the train station cloak room.

Lady Bracknell tells Jack that he can never attain a respectable position in society having been found in a cloak room and raised by a man in the country. Jack is at a lost, and asks Lady Bracknell what he must do so that he can marry Gwendolyn. Lady Bracknell says in order to become respectable, he must procure relations as soon as possible, and ideally have parents with strong lineages by the end of the season.

Jack tells Lady Bracknell that what she asks of him is impossible. He tells her that he can procure the handbag he was found in, and she is offended. Jack doesn't understand why it matters if he was found in a handbag, and Lady Bracknell responds that Gwendolyn is her only daughter, raised with utmost care and that she will not allow her to wed anyone with a questionable background. She gets up and leaves the room in a huff.

When she is gone, Algernon begins playing the wedding march from the other room. Jack is angry and tells him to stop. Algernon is in high spirits because he assumes that Gwendolyn refused Jack, but Jack tells him that it was her mother who refused him. Jack calls Lady Bracknell a monster, and Algernon is delighted to hear his relations abused. Jack once again reprimands him for being overly cynical, and wonders if Gwendolyn will end up like her mother when she is old.

Algernon cleverly responds that all women end up like their mothers, and all men don't, and it is tragedy on both accounts. Jack says he is tired of cleverness and wishes the world were full of fools. Algernon says the world is full of fools, and that the fools talk of the clever people. Algernon deftly changes the subject back to Jack's dilemma, and asks if he revealed to Gwendolyn the truth about his name. Jack says he hadn't, but he still plans on killing Ernest off. Cecily will be upset, but she will be fine.

Algernon expresses interest in meeting Cecily, and Jack forbids it, the reason being Cecily is pretty and only eighteen. Algernon asks if Gwendolyn will approve of him having a beautiful eighteen year old ward, and Jack declares that the two of them will be sisters.

It is almost seven, and if they want a reservation for dinner, they'll have to get ready. After dinner Algernon wants to go to the theatre or the club, but Jack says he would rather do nothing. He is obviously upset about Gwendolyn's mother still.

Lane enters the room and introduces Miss Fairfax. Gwendolyn comes in and tells Algernon to turn around because she wishes to talk to Ernest. Algernon protests, but after some banter sits turned around and pretends to read a magazine.

Jack is surprised to see Gwendolyn but happy. Gwendolyn reveals that she fears the two will never be married. However, she has heard about Jack's story from her mother, and it has inspired her eternal devotion to Jack. She says he fascinates her, and that even if she marries someone else she will always be his. Gwendolyn has his town address, but also wants to know his address in the country. Jack gladly gives it. We see Algernon, who is listening closely to their conversation, write the address on the inside of his shirtsleeve before pretending to read again.

Gwendolyn promises to send Jack letters every day and wants to know how much longer he will be in town. Jack tells her he will be in town until Monday. Their conversation being over, Gwendolyn tells Algernon he can turn around now, and Algernon replies he already has. Jack offers to walk Gwendolyn back to her carriage, and the two exit.

Lane enters the room with several letters on a silver tray. Algernon examines them before tearing them up and declaring to Lane that he will be bun-burying this weekend. He asks Lane to get him some sherry, and to pack his bunbury clothes. Lane asks when Algernon is planning on returning to town, and Algernon says he will come back Monday (the same day Jack is leaving town). He hopes the weather to be fine, to which Lane replies it never is. Algernon compliments Lane on being a perfect pessimist and Lane sarcastically replies that his only wish is to please.

Jack comes back, his mood improved, to find Algernon laughing. When Jack asks what he is laughing about, Algernon tells him he is anxious for Bunbury's health. Jack recommends that Algernon get rid of Bunbury for good before he gets into trouble. Algernon, however, enjoys trouble. Jack accuses Algernon of being filled with nonsense and leaves. Algernon sits down, lights a cigarette, looks at the address written on his cuff sleeve, and smiles.

Act II

The scene takes place in the garden of the manor house. It is July, and the garden and decorations are old-fashioned and quaint. Miss Prism is sitting at the table, and Cecily is watering the flowers.

Miss Prism tells Cecily that watering flowers is a waste of time and that she needs to come study her German. Cecily doesn't like German and says it is unbecoming. Her guardian, Uncle Jack, however, stresses that she learn it. Cecily tells Miss Prism that Uncle Jack is too serious, and Miss Prism defends him, citing his admirable duty and responsible nature. Cecily still thinks Jack seems bored at home with them, and Miss Prism attributes that to the stress of having to worry about his trouble-making brother, Ernest.

Cecily thinks it would good to meet Ernest and thinks that maybe they could be a strong influence on him. Miss Prism, however, thinks Ernest is far too wicked to be helped.

Cecily begins writing in her diary, and Miss Prism asks why she insists on writing. Cecily answers that she doesn't want to forget the marvellous secrets of her life. Miss Prism believes that is what memory is for. Cecily argues with Miss Prism again, saying that memory is responsible for too many novels. She doesn't like novels that end happily, as they make her depressed.

The two see Doctor Chasuble entering the garden. Doctor Chasuble greets Miss Prism and Cecily, and Cecily suggests that the two take a stroll around the garden. Miss Prism tells Cecily that she is just trying to get out of studying, and Cecily openly admits not being an attentive learner.

Doctor Chasuble and Miss Prism obviously like each other, and nervously flirt. The two decide to take a walk, and when the exit the stage Cecily angrily throws her books on the table.

Merriman, the house-servant enters with a letter of introduction for Ernest Worthington who has arrived with his luggage and is waiting outside. "Ernest" has been informed that Jack is in town and wishes to speak to Cecily instead. Cecily orders Merriman to prepare a room for their guest, and to send him in.

She is nervous and thinks to herself that she has never met anyone wicked before. She is afraid he will look just like everyone else.

Algernon enters the garden, and Cecily thinks he does look like a normal person. He greets her as his little cousin Cecily. She tartly responds that she isn't little and is tall for her age. Algernon is taken aback, but she continues on to say that she is Cecily, and he must be her wicked cousin Ernest.

Algernon tells her he isn't wicket at all. Cecily tells him that would be dreadfully dull, and that he better not be living a double life, pretending to be wicked when he's actually good. Algernon is amazed at Cecily, and gladly tells her that he has, in fact, been reckless recently.

Cecily is glad that he is upholding his reputation for being a troublemaker, but tells him that Uncle Jack won't be back in the country until Monday. Algernon says he has an appointment in London that he cannot miss, so he won't be able to stay until Uncle Jack gets back. Cecily teases him, saying that Uncle Jack is getting ready to emigrate him and is off buying him an outfit to be sent off in. Algernon tells her that he wouldn't allow Jack to buy him clothes, as Jack has horrible taste. Cecily continues teasing, saying he won't need neckties as he's being sent to Australia.

Her joke came from a comment Uncle Jack made a few nights ago, about Ernest choosing this world, the next world, or Australia. Algernon tells Cecily that Australia and the next world are equally bad, and he'd prefer to stay in this one if possible.

Cecily tells him that he isn't good enough to stay in this world, and he asks for her help in reforming himself. She replies that she doesn't have time this afternoon, but he is welcome to give it a try if he wants.

She invites him in for food, and he picks a flower for his buttonhole. He flirtingly compares her to the flower, and Cecily tells him that is inappropriate talk, and that Miss Prism doesn't think beauty is worth all that much. Algernon says beauty is what will ensnare any sensible man, and Cecily says it's just as well, because she wouldn't know what to do with a sensible man.

They exit into the manor, presumably continuing their flirtatious banter. When they exit the stage, Miss Prism and Doctor Chasuble enter.

Miss Prism is telling the Chasuble that he is too alone, and that he should get married. It can be inferred from their conversation that the Doctor is a priest and cannot marry because of his religious order. Miss Prism tells him that the old ways need to be discarded and that having a single man around all the time is a temptation.

The Chasuble asks if married men are not attractive, and Miss Prism replies that they are only attractive to their wives. The Chasuble responds that often they aren't even then. Miss Prism states that it depends entirely on the woman. Maturity is to be trusted, and young girls are "green" (unripe). The Chasuble is startled at her frankness, and she apologizes, stating that it was just a metaphor.

Their conversation is cut off when Jack enters the garden, dressed entirely in black, and acting as though he is in mourning. Miss Prism and the Chasuble immediately ask him what is the matter, and Jack tells them gravel that his brother Ernest is dead. He died of a severe chill in Paris, and wishes to be buried there. The Chasuble offers to mention him in his Sunday service.

Jack is reminded by the Chasuble and asks if he can perform christenings. The Chasuble misunderstands, thinking he is talking about an infant, but Jack clarifies that it is he who wishes to be christened. He is concerned that he is too old to be christened, but the Chasuble assures him that no age is too old and that he can indeed perform the ceremony.

They set a time at five in the afternoon for the service, and the Chasuble says that he is doing twins at the same time. Jack thinks it would seem silly to be christened at the same time as infants, and they settle on five-thirty.

Miss Prism is glad that such a blessed event is the result of such a tragedy (Ernest's death). Just then, Cecily enters the garden and greets Uncle Jack. As soon as she's done greeting him, she tells him to change out of his horrid black clothes. When Uncle Jack acts morose, she asks him what is the matter, but before he can answer she tells him she has a tremendous surprise for him, that his brother Ernest has come for a visit and is waiting in the dining room.

Jack is astounded, and Cecily assures him that he arrived half an hour ago with his luggage in tow. Jack tells her he hasn't got a brother, which Miss Prism and the Chasuble assume to mean Ernest is dead, and Cecily assumes Jack has disowned him. She tells Jack that he cannot disown his own brother, even if he is wicked. She offers to go get him and leaves the scene.

The Chasuble is joyful at the sudden turn-around, but Miss Prism seems distressed. Jack is confused, until Algernon and Cecily enter the garden walking hand-in-hand. Jack is upset and tries to get Algernon away from Cecily.

Algernon tells Jack he is sorry for all the trouble, and that he intends to be a reformed man. Jack glares at him, and refuses to shake his hand. Cecily reprimands Jack, who says "Ernest" is a disgrace, and he will never shake his hand.

Cecily is mortified that Jack would treat his own brother so. She tells Jack about Algernon's devotion to his deal invalid friend Bunbury and that if he visits someone so ill he could hardly be considered bad.

Jack responds that "Ernest" is not allowed to talk to Cecily about anything. Algernon guilt trips him, saying his coldness is painful. Cecily is so outraged that she says she will never forgive Jack if he doesn't shake Algernon's hand. Jack does so reluctantly, glaring the entire time. The Chasuble and Cecily admire the "brotherly reunion" and leave them alone.

Jack accuses Algernon of being a scoundrel and forbids any Bunburying at his manor. Merriman enters and informs Jack that he put "Ernest's" luggage in his room. Jack is incredulous, and orders Algernon to leave at once, telling Merriman that he was suddenly ordered back to town. Algernon calls Jack a liar and says he didn't hear anyone calling him. Jack says his duty as a gentleman is calling him.

Algernon changes the subject to Cecily, and Jack forbids him to talk of her. Algernon makes fun of Jack, telling him that his clothes are ridiculous. Jack is getting more and more angry, and orders Algernon to leave again. Algernon says he won't leave while Jack is in mourning because it would be unkind. Jack says he'll go change his clothes, and Algernon makes fun of him again for taking too long to dress. Jack makes fun of Algernon for always being overdressed, and Algernon replies he makes up for it by being overeducated. Jack yells at Algernon that he is absurd and that he must leave immediately before exiting the scene.

Algernon admits to himself that he is in love with Cecily, and will do anything to see her again. He sees her watering flowers in the garden. She wonders where Uncle Jack is, and Algernon tells her that Jack is kicking him out of the house. Cecily is upset at being parted after just meeting.

Merriman enters, saying the cart is ready. Cecily tells him to give them five more minutes, and Merriman leaves.

Algernon tells Cecily that she is absolute perfection and Cecily tells him to pause because she's going to copy it in her diary. She tells him to continue, and, surprised, he goes on a short monologue saying how much he loves her.

Merriman comes in again and says the cart is ready. Algernon tells him to have the cart come back in a week. Cecily says Jack will be mad, but Algernon doesn't care, all he wants is to marry Cecily. She tells him that they have been engaged for three months now and that she fell madly in love with him after hearing all the stories about his wickedness. She settled the engagement herself, buying rings and bracelets, and even wrote love letters between the two of them.

Algernon has a small scare when Cecily says the engagement was broken off a month ago, and pleads with Cecily to take him back because he didn't do anything wrong. He recovers when Cecily reveals that all serious engagements must be broken at least once and that she forgave him a week later. He calls her an angel and kisses her, and she runs her hand through his hair. He makes her promise never to break off their engagement again, and she says she can't now that she's met him. And, of course, there is the matter of his name. She has always admired the name Ernest, and pities any woman who doesn't marry a man with such a strong, confident name.

Algernon asks if she would love him if his name wasn't Ernest, but, in fact, Algernon. Cecily replies that she doesn't like the name, and she could respect someone named Algernon, but not love him. Algernon tries to defend his own name, to no avail. He says he must go see the rector immediately, and that he'll be back in half an hour. She says that is too soon, and he promises twenty minutes. He kisses her and leaves.

Cecily enters his proposal in her diary. Merriman comes in, saying that a Miss Fairfax has come to call on Mr. Worthing on a matter of urgent business. Cecily thinks he is in the library, but Merriman says he has gone to the rectory. Cecily tells him to bring Miss Fairfax and tea.

Gwendolyn enters, and they introduce themselves. Gwendolyn says she likes Cecily's name, and that she always hopes to call her by her first name, but only if Cecily will do the same for her. Cecily agrees, and politely asks Gwendolyn to sit.

Gwendolyn tells Cecily that her father is Lord Bracknell and asks if she has heard of him. Cecily hasn't, and apologizes. Gwendolyn says it's okay, and that he isn't well-known outside the family circle. She asks if it is okay for her to look at Cecily through her glasses, and Cecily replies that she is fond of being looked at.

Gwendolyn examines her and says surely she is here at this manor on a short visit. Cecily tells her that she lives here, and Gwendolyn is shocked. She wants to know if any older female relations also live here, but Cecily says the only other woman is her governess, Miss Prism. Cecily tells Gwendolyn that she has no relations and is Mr. Worthing's ward.

Gwendolyn speaks frankly, saying that she wished Cecily were older and more plain so as not to tempt her upright and moral Ernest to stray. Cecily says there has been a misunderstanding, and that she is John Worthing's ward, Ernest's older brother. Gwendolyn is suspicious as to why she's never heard of John before, and Cecily tells her that the brothers have not been on good relations, but have just only recently been reunited.

She seems happy at this news, and makes sure once again that Cecily is not Ernest Worthing's ward. Cecily says there is no way she could be his ward, as she is engaged to Ernest Worthing. Gwendolyn is outraged and tells Cecily that it is, in fact, she who is engaged to Ernest.

As proof of the engagement, Cecily shows Gwendolyn her diary, which she wrote not ten minutes ago. Gwendolyn also produces a diary of her own and shows Cecily Ernest's proposal at five-thirty the previous afternoon. She says that because he proposed to her first, she has first claim. Cecily says that if he proposed to her today, then he's obviously changed his mind about Gwendolyn.

The two girls begin slinging insults at one another. Gwendolyn accuses Cecily of entrapping Ernest into an engagement, and Cecily tells Gwendolyn she is nothing more than an entanglement.

Merriman comes in with tea and sets the table. The two are silent, and then engage in tense small-talk. Gwendolyn asks if there are any amusing walks around, and Cecily tells her that from the hilltops you can see five different countries. Gwendolyn pretends not to be impressed, saying that it seems rather crowded. Cecily retorts that must be the reason Gwendolyn lives in town.

At this point, Gwendolyn is extremely nervous. She is biting her lip and tapping her foot. She tells Cecily that the manor garden is well kept but that she could never live in the country without being bored.

Cecily offers her tea, and Gwendolyn politely thanks her. In an aside, she expresses her distaste for Cecily.

When Cecily asks her if she likes sugar in her tea, Gwendolyn replies that it isn't fashionable to drink sugar anymore. Cecily puts four lumps of sugar in Gwendolyn's cup. She asks if Gwendolyn would like bread and butter or cake with her tea and Gwendolyn says that she prefers bread and butter, as cake isn't seen in the best houses nowadays. Cecily gives her a small slice of cake.

When Gwendolyn drinks her tea and sees the cake, she is outraged. She stands and tells Cecily that she has gone too far. Cecily replies that she will go to any length to keep Ernest away from her.

They begin hurling personal insults again. Gwendolyn professes to have immediately distrusted Cecily, and Cecily coldly hints that Gwendolyn surely has other engagements to go to.

While the girls are staring each other down, Jack enters the scene. Gwendolyn shouts his name, Ernest, and runs to him. They greet each other passionately. Gwendolyn asks Jack is he is engaged to Cecily, and he laughs before saying that he is not.

Cecily interrupts their passionate reunion by revealing "Ernest's" true name to be John. Gwendolyn backs away from him, distrusting.

Algernon walks in and goes straight to Cecily. She asks him if he is engaged to Gwendolyn, and he starts, not expecting to see her at the manor. He tells Cecily he isn't engaged, and the two kiss. Gwendolyn reveals him to be her cousin, Algernon, and it is Cecily's turn to back away.

The two girls hug each other, stricken. They ask the men if it is true, if neither of them are actually Ernest. The men admit their true names, and say they have nothing to be ashamed of. The girls apologize for accusing each other earlier, and console one another at the men's deceit. The men pace the garden, frustrated at the girls' camaraderie.

Cecily and Gwendolyn ask where Ernest is as they are both engaged to a man they have never met and want to get this matter settled once and for all. Jack tells the truth, that he doesn't have a brother named Ernest, that he made him up.

The girls realize that they aren't engaged to anyone, and Cecily remarks that it isn't a pleasant situation to find oneself in. Gwendolyn suggests they go into the house because the men won't dare to follow them. They leave, arm in arm, giving the men scornful looks as they leave the garden.

Jack turns to Algernon, and asks sarcastically if he is satisfied with the trouble his Bunburying has brought. Algernon, falsely cheerful, replies that this is the most exciting Bunbury he has ever gone on. Jack tells him that he had no right to Bunbury at his country manor, and Algernon says he has the right to Bunbury anywhere, and that any serious Bunburyist knows that to be a fact.

Jack throws up his hands in frustration, and expresses that the only decent thing to come out of this whole mess is that Bunbury is gone. Algernon reminds Jack that his brother Ernest is gone as well, and he will no longer have a convenient excuse go to town whenever he likes.

The two express that their only wish is to be engaged to the women inside, and they also tell each other that there is no chance of that happening, because Cecily is Jack's ward and Gwendolyn Algernon's cousin. Both men are being overprotective of their relations, and won't allow the other to court them.

Algernon sits down and begins calmly eating muffins. Jack calls him heartless for eating at such a time, to which Algernon replies that eating consoles him in times of stress and that he has a particular fondness for muffins. Jack takes the muffins away and tells Algernon to eat the tea-cakes.

When Algernon protests that he doesn't like tea cakes, Jack tells him to leave. Algernon refuses to leave without dinner and says he is scheduled to be christened under the name of Ernest. Jack tells Algernon that he is already scheduled and that they can't both be Ernest. He reminds Algernon that he has already been christened, and can't be again. Jack picks up the muffin tray, and Algernon is upset because there are only two muffins left.

Jack once again tells Algernon to leave, and Algernon once again refuses, saying he must finish his muffins. Jack groans and sits down, and Algernon eats his muffins.

Act III

The third scene opens inside the manor house. Cecily and Gwendolyn are looking out the window at the men in the garden and talking about their behavior.

Gwendolyn says that the fact that they didn't follow shows that they have some shame about the way they've acted, and Cecily notices that they are eating muffins reproachfully. It is obvious that they want to forgive the boys but that they don't want to lose their pride.

Gwendolyn tells Cecily to give a cough, so as to attract their attention. When they do look, however, she expresses disgust at their forwardness. Cecily points out that they are coming towards the house, and Gwendolyn says that they must maintain a dignified silence. On no account are Cecily and Gwendolyn going to be the first to speak.

When the men enter whistling a popular song, Gwendolyn immediately tells Jack that she has a question for him. Cecily asks Algernon why he pretended to be Jack's brother Ernest, and Algernon replies that he just wanted to meet her. Cecily asks Gwendolyn if his answer was satisfactory, and Gwendolyn says yes, if she believes it. Cecily doesn't believe it, but acknowledges that it was still a decent answer. Gwendolyn agrees and asks Jack why he pretended to be Ernest. Jack tells her he wanted an excuse to go to town as often as possible to see her.

The girls confer among themselves about the replies, and say that they seem to be true. Gwendolyn wonders if it is okay to forgive them, and Cecily says it is, then quickly changes her mind. Gwendolyn understands at once, and asks Cecily if she wants to bring up the critical issue together. Gwendolyn taps the time, and then the two say in unison that the men's Christian names are an insurmountable issue. The men reply back, in unison, that they have already scheduled appointments to be christened.

Gwendolyn affirms this with Jack, and Cecily with Algernon. They are delighted that the men would go to such lengths to please them. Gwendolyn praises their self-sacrifice and Cecily their courage. The couples fall into each other's arms.

Merriman enters and coughs, announcing the arrival of Lady Bracknell. The couples separate in alarm, and Lady Bracknell walks in. She immediately reprimands Gwendolyn for running away to see Mr. Worthing and Gwendolyn boldly announces that she is engaged to him. Lady Bracknell is upset, and orders Gwendolyn to her before turning on Mr. Worthing. She tells the group that she found out of Gwendolyn's flight from her maid, and that Mr. Worthing must cease all communication with Gwendolyn immediately.

Jack tells Lady Bracknell that it is too late; they are already in love and promised to one another. Lady Bracknell once again asserts that it is impossible. She notices Algernon, and asks him if this is his invalid friend, Bunbury's house.

Algernon stammers out that he killed Bunbury this afternoon, and quickly corrects himself, saying instead that Bunbury died. When Lady Bracknell asks what he died of, Algernon says he exploded. Lady Bracknell is confused, but Algernon assures her that Bunbury is dead, and that's all that matters. She is glad he made up his mind to finally die and asks Algernon who the girl he is holding is.

Jack interjects, saying Cecily is his ward. Lady Bracknell coldly greets Cecily. Algernon and Cecily announce their engagement to Lady Bracknell, who sits down on the sofa in shock. She inquires about Cecily's past, and wonders if she has any connection to the railway Jack was found in. Jack is furious at her implications but restrains himself. He tells her that Cecily is the grand-daughter of Thomas Cardew, and when she asks for proof of this he tells her he is in possession of all Cecily's records from the time she was a child.

Lady Bracknell has heard enough, and decided that Cecily is not a suitable match for Algernon. She rises to leave, and orders Gwendolyn to come with her. Before she leaves, she asks about Cecily's inheritance, and Jack reveals that it is quite a fortune. Lady Bracknell sits back down and reassesses Cecily, saying that so few women today are suitable matches because of their lack of fortune. She remarks that Cecily is indeed pretty and asks her to come closer. Lady Bracknell examines Cecily from all angles before declaring that her profile has social possibilities.

Algernon tells his Aunt that he doesn't care about Cecily's "social possibilities" because she is perfect in every way. At this, Lady Bracknell gives them consent to marry and tells Cecily to call her Aunt Augusta from now on. Cecily and Algernon both thank Lady Bracknell, who goes on to say that the marriage should take place as soon as possible, so that the two don't get to know each other's character too well before marriage.

Jack interrupts their happy planning; reminding everyone that Cecily is his ward and cannot marry until she comes of age. Lady Bracknell asks Jack on what grounds would he refuse Algernon, and Jack says Algernon has no moral character and is known to be untruthful. Lady Bracknell vehemently assures Jack that Algernon has strong moral character.

Jack goes on a tangent, saying that Algernon came to his house under false pretenses, drank his best wine, and ate all the muffins at tea. Lady Bracknell doesn't think these offenses are worthy of refusing marriage and asks Cecily how old she is. Cecily replies that she is eighteen, but admits to twenty at evening parties. Lady Bracknell says she will come of age soon, and that they can hold off the marriage until then. Jack once again interrupts, saying that Thomas Cardew's will doesn't allow her to come of age until thirty-five.

This hurdle is once again avoided by Lady Bracknell, who states that thirty-five is a attractive age, and hints that Cecily's fortune will have gained quite a bit from interest by then. She tells the couple that they can still marry. Cecily asks Algernon if he would wait for her, and he assures her that he would. Cecily, however, says she hates waiting. Algernon asks her, lamenting at their situation, what they should do.

Lady Bracknell urges Jack to reconsider his decision. Jack tells Lady Bracknell that if she gives him consent to marry Gwendolyn, then he will give consent to Algernon to marry Cecily. Lady Bracknell is outraged at this suggestion and says that it is impossible. She tells Gwendolyn they must leave immediately.

Dr. Chasuble enters, saying that the preparations have been made for the christenings. Lady Bracknell misunderstands, thinking the couples are already planning on having children. The matter is cleared up when the Chasuble says the christenings are for Jack and Algernon. Lady Bracknell forbids them to be christened, saying it is improper. The Chasuble asks Jack if he doesn't want to be christened, and Jack replies that, in his current situation, christening wouldn't do him any good.

The Chasuble then says if he doesn't have any baptisms to perform, then he is going to return to Miss Prism, who has been waiting for him at the church. Lady Bracknell becomes alert when the Chasuble mentions Miss Prism and asks the Chasuble to describe her and her position in his household, saying it is a matter of vital importance. The Chasuble describes Miss Prism as a lady of cultivation and respect, and tells Lady Bracknell that he is celibate.

Jack reveals Miss Prism to be Cecily's governess of the past three years. Lady Bracknell becomes severe and says she must see Miss Prism at once. The Chasuble looks outside, and notices Miss Prism is approaching the house.

Miss Prism enters and tells the Chasuble that she has been waiting for him for almost an hour. She sees Lady Bracknell and suddenly goes terribly pale. Lady Bracknell yells at Miss Prism to come to her, and Miss Prism approaches, shaking.

Lady Bracknell questions Miss Prism, asking her what happened to the baby. Everyone in the room is staring with rapt attention at the scandal unfolding. Lady Bracknell goes on to say that 28 years ago Miss Prism was charged with looking after a baby boy at Lord Bracknell's house. She left with the baby, and later the police found the carriage with a three-volume manuscript in it, but no baby. Lady Bracknell asks Miss Prism again what happened to the boy.

Miss Prism pauses, then, ashamed, tells the story. When she was charged with looking after the boy, she had a terrible cold, and her head was fuzzy. When she went out, taking the baby with her, she accidentally placed the baby in her handbag instead of her manuscript. When she realized her mistake, she ran away.

Jack asks where she left the handbag, and Miss Prism replies vaguely that she doesn't remember. Jack insists that she tell him, saying it is of utmost importance. Miss Prism admits that she left the handbag in the cloak-room of a railway station.

Jack turns to Gwendolyn, asking her to excuse him, but he must go to his room for a minute. Gwendolyn, overdramatic, tells Jack that she will wait for him all her life for him to come back to her. Jack rushes out of the room, flushed with excitement and agitation.

Doctor Chasuble demands to know the meaning of his behavior, and Lady Bracknell tells him she doesn't even want to suspect. The group hears noises from upstairs, as if someone is moving trunks. Cecily wonders why Uncle Jack is so agitated, and the Chasuble tells her he has an emotional nature. The noises stop, and then redouble. Lady Bracknell hopes it will end soon, and Gwendolyn says she can't stand the suspense, though she wants it to last.

Finally, Jack runs back downstairs, carrying a black handbag. He asks Miss Prism if this is the handbag she left in the cloak-room, and to examine it closely before answering. Miss Prism points to her initials on the purse, and is gladly surprised to have it returned to her after all these years. Jack tells her in a pathetic voice that he was the baby she placed in the handbag. Miss Prism is shocked as Jack calls her mother and tries to embrace her. She tells Jack that she is unmarried and has no children but that Lady Bracknell can tell him who his mother is.

Lady Bracknell reveals Jack to be the son of her sister, and Algernon's older brother. Jack, ecstatic, hugs Algy, telling him that he must act like a brother from here on out. The two shake hands. Gwendolyn reminds Jack that the issue of his Christian name still hasn't been solved, and Jack says in the excitement of finding out his origins, he forgot all about it. He asks Lady Bracknell if he was christened as an infant, and she says yes. He was named after his father. Impatiently, Jack wants to know what his father's name was, but Lady Bracknell cannot recall. He asks Algernon, but Algy was only one year old when their father died, so he doesn't remember his Christian name.

Jack thinks and goes over to the old army records. He finds his father, whose Christian name was Ernest John. Lady Bracknell comments that now she remembers why she always disliked the name Ernest, but Jack and Gwendolyn are ecstatic.

Jack apologizes to Gwendolyn, saying it is a terrible thing to find out he has been being truthful all the time and hopes she will forgive him. She does, and they embrace lovingly. Everyone is happy, and the Chasuble embraces Miss Prism, and Algernon embraces Cecily. Jack says he finally realizes the Importance of Being Ernest.

The Life and Times of Oscar Wilde

Times of Oscar Wilde

Oscar Wilde was born in the Victorian era. Queen Victoria had been on the throne of Great Britain, Ireland, and the British Commonwealth for almost two decades when Wilde was born in Dublin in 1854. Ireland was still under British rule and the Republic of Ireland would not achieve its independence for many decades. The author died two months before Victoria did, on 30 November 1900.

The Victorian era was a time of great change. The Industrial Revolution, beginning at the end of the 1800's, had fomented change in working conditions, work hours, and social classes. The changes in work and opportunities created a larger middle class and by the end of the Victorian era, it had grown to include a significant percentage of the population of the British Isles.

Oscar Wilde's Anglo-Irish family would have been considered to be of the upper class. In those times in Great Britain and Ireland, members of the upper class were not necessary wealthy. The distinction was often one of land ownership, religious denomination, education, and "breeding" (which meant belonging to a family with deep roots in the upper class). Wilde's parents came from the right background (mostly English and Anglican) and Oscar's father was a respected doctor.

Although the Wilde family was considered eccentric and "arty", Oscar's parents and other relatives would have been the products of their background and well acquainted with its structure. It was a society where everyone, or almost everyone, "knew their place". Later in life Wilde was to challenge the conventional sexual mores of Victorian Britain, and would pay a heavy price. His homosexual practices would have been abhorrent to most members of the middle and upper class – and while it was hardly a novel orientation, it was not something "respectable" people would flaunt.

There was hypocrisy present in Victorian society – houses of prostitution existed, men kept mistresses, women were not always faithful to their husbands, couples lived apart, and homosexuality was practiced, but the great majority of people preferred to ignore such issues and sweep them under the carpet. They were not talked about in polite company. Homosexuals were relegated to the fringes of society but if they chose not to live on the fringes, they were forced to live a lie or to doing their utmost to disguise their orientation.

Family life and church going were considered commendable pursuits for most people, especially the burgeoning middle classes. While the upper class could escape some of the stricter conventions, they were increasingly under the scrutiny of the popular press. Society was becoming more literate and newspapers and magazines were multiplying – the peccadilloes of the upper class entertained and titillated the middle and lower classes.

The world that Oscar Wilde moved in, especially after he left Dublin, was philosophically modelled on the Aesthetic Movement, which had begun in the 18th century and championed "art for art's sake". Art existed as a separate entity – it was not created merely for pleasure or bothered by the restraints of morality or practical application. Wilde was a great leader in this movement at the end of the 19th century and he moved within a circle of artists, writers, thinkers, and hedonists who supported this philosophy. Many of these people were freed from the restraints of having to make a living – it was a philosophy that suited those with leisure time, ample private funds, and, at the time, belonging to the male sex.

Women were still expected to toe the line in their day to day lives. Wilde's adherence to the Aesthetic movement probably influenced his decision to cast off his conventional marriage and live openly as a homosexual in an age when it was unusual for a prominent person to do so.

Wilde's family background – brilliant, bohemian, accomplished, and eccentric – cushioned him in a sense. He had grown up around people who were not conventional. He witnessed his own father embroiled in a sex scandal.

Oscar had several illegitimate half-siblings, which were acknowledged openly by his father; a rather rare occurrence in conservative heavily Roman Catholic Ireland. His mother was not the typical mother of any class – she was educated, a rebellious political activist, and later led a *salon* of thinkers and creative people in London.

Wilde came of age in this unconventional atmosphere. When he reached adulthood, and settled in London, he surrounded himself with people from the fringes of society, and kicked back at the conventional hypocrisies of Victorian England. When Wilde challenged an establishment icon he had to deal with the catastrophic results which ruined his career and probably shortened his life. His unconventional life was no match for the establishment of Victorian Britain.

Family of Oscar Wilde

There can be little doubt that Oscar Wilde, whose very name conjures up the spectre of Victorian morality, was born into a very unusual family. Oscar was one of three children. He had an older brother, William, and a younger sister Isola.

Wilde was born in Dublin, Ireland in 1854. His family was Anglo-Irish in origin. The Anglo-Irish were mainly Protestant – usually Anglican – and had connections to England; usually through ancestors who had come to Ireland to form the ruling class. They were part of an elite group – not necessarily very wealthy, but often among the educated and privileged of a pre-Independent Ireland.

Oscar's father, William Robert Wills Wilde, was a doctor as his father had been before him. William's father had been a well-regarded country physician in County Roscommon but it was his son who would rise to eminence in his field. William Wilde (who was knighted in 1864) was an ophthalmologist, and despite not completing a college degree, had an M.D. bestowed upon him by Dublin University while in his early twenties.

In 1837 he completed his training as a surgeon and in that year, he also published an article on literature. Within a few years he had founded St. Mark's Ophthalmic Hospital in Dublin. He continued to write on a number of subjects, including antiquities, Jonathan Swift, and medicine. He was recognized for his work on statistics and received several honorary degrees from European universities.

The King of Sweden gave him the Order of the Polar Star – and later became one of son Oscar's godfathers. Sir William was prominent in helping preserve Irish folklore and published works on the ancient history of Ireland. In 1864 he was knighted after he served as an Irish Census Commissioner and gathered valuable data and statistics on the deaf and mute.

Sir William was not without his faults. He is said to have had a weakness for alcohol, which he passed on to Oscar. Sir William married in his mid-thirties, but not before he had fathered three illegitimate children. Sir William had a reputation as a womanizer, and there were rumors about his involvement with women, including the Queen of Sweden.

At least one patient, possibly actually his mistress, claimed that he had raped her while she was under the influence of chloroform. This accusation actually led to a court case, foreshadowing his son's later troubles, and it was settled in the favor of his accuser and Wilde had to part with £2000 in legal fees.

Sir William Wilde died in Dublin in 1876, at the age of 61. Overshadowed by his son's fame and notoriety, he nevertheless left a legacy of accomplishment.

Oscar Wilde's mother was also an interesting and accomplished person in her own right. Born Jane Francesca Elgee in 1821 (she later habitually made herself five years younger than she actually was) in Wexford, she was the great-granddaughter of an English bricklayer who had immigrated to Ireland.

His son became an Archdeacon in the Anglican Church and his grandson, Jane's father, became a successful lawyer. She counted among her relatives a prominent Arctic explorer, Robert McClure. Jane was to suffer from her father's absenteeism as he suddenly left for India when she was very small and died there in 1825.

Jane claimed to have Italian blood and that the Elgee name was a corruption of an Italian surname. She spoke several languages, quoted Aeschylus, and had little interest in running a household: the Wilde home was often dirty and messy. It is said that Oscar Wilde inherited his imposing height and posture from his mother.

As a young woman Jane published poetry in one of Ireland's national publications, *The Nation*. She used the pen name "Sperenza" and was assumed to be a man until she revealed herself to the editor as a woman. Jane, inspired by the nationalist writing published by *The Nation* later immersed herself in Irish Nationalism, supporting the country's independence from Great Britain.

Although she had been born into a Protestant, and by her own description Conservative family, the plight of the Catholic Nationalists appealed to her emotions and inspired her to poetry. As Lady Wilde, her prominence gave her political views some clout and no doubt encouraged the Nationalist movement. In 1848 she wrote an article for *The Nation* that supported violence for the cause of independence – meanwhile her editor, Gavin Duffy, who had first published her poems, languished in jail.

The edition that contained her article was suppressed – and no doubt Jane's position of a woman of the Anglo-Protestant establishment protected her. She and another woman took on the editing of *The Nation* while Duffy was in jail.

With such a background, it was no wonder that Oscar Wilde went on to become such a talented and prolific writer and his unconventional upbringing may have also contributed to his downfall.

Childhood and Education of Oscar Wilde

Oscar Fingal O'Flahertie Wills Wilde was born on October 16th, 1854 (although Wilde liked to subtract a few years from his age, just as his mother did) in Dublin, Ireland. He was named for his godfather (the King of Sweden), for figures in Irish folklore, and for his father.

The Wilde family relocated soon after his birth to Merrion Square, Dublin, where his sister Isola was born in 1856. Isola died when she was only eight years old and Oscar felt her loss keenly. He later wrote a poem in her memory, *Requiescat*. Wilde also had an older brother William, known as Willie.

Oscar was born when his father was almost forty and enjoying a successful career as a doctor and antiquarian. His mother was an accomplished and respected poet and activist. Their young son was educated at home as a young boy; the norm for one of his background. It wasn't long, though, before he was sent away to school, which was also normal for a lad from the upper class.

Oscar attended Portora Royal School in Enniskillen, Fermanagh, Ireland, later to be included in Northern Ireland when the Republic of Ireland became an independent nation. It is unlikely that Wilde mixed much with the Irish Catholic boys of his own age – their backgrounds, in religious and social terms, would have been poles apart.

In later years, when he had left Ireland for good, his unconventional Anglo-Irish background must have been viewed as somewhat exotic by the English of Victorian England.

Oscar seems to have shown flair at an early age. In a letter to his mother he wrote when he was only 13 years old, he described two of his flannel shirts as being "scarlet" and "lilac" in color. It is said that Lady Wilde, who had hoped her second child would be female, had dressed young Oscar as a girl when he was small.

Oscar did not have many friends as a child, probably a result of his "different" background and his brilliance. It is impossible to know if he felt homosexual feelings while still a school boy, but it is certainly likely he felt different from the other boys around him. In any case, he did well academically. He took the top prize for Classics during his last two years and also took a second prize for Drawing.

In 1871 Oscar won the Royal School Scholarship to the prestigious Anglo-Irish institution, Trinity College, in Dublin. There he was mentored by John Pentland Mahaffy, whom he referred to as his "first and greatest teacher". Oscar also met Edward Carson at Trinity, an academic rival, whom Wilde beat out for a scholarship and an academic medal. Carson, who was born in Dublin and was of Scottish background, became a lawyer and would later prosecute Wilde in court, leading to Oscar's imprisonment.

Wilde's religious views as an atheist were not appreciated in 19th century Ireland and would certainly not have been popular at the Church of England-run Trinity College. He suffered jeers and criticism from his contemporaries due to his lack of belief in God.

Oscar remained at Trinity College for three years and did brilliantly. He then won another scholarship, this time to Magdalen College at Oxford – a university with as illustrious a reputation in the 19th century as it has today. Wilde was about to embark on his adult life, with all its brilliance and its tragedy – and in the main, he was to leave Ireland behind.

Wilde continued to shock, even in a more liberal England. His religious views were not suffered gladly at Oxford and he gained a reputation for flamboyant dress and manners. Was Wilde only honestly expressing himself or was he seeking a way to create a self-identity?

His attention getting ways may point to insecurity – as he later said "There is only one thing in the world that is worse than being talked about, and that is not being talked about" – in other words, any attention was better than no attention. Whatever his reasons, Wilde was noticed. He collected blue china and feathers and affected velvet knee-breeches, which might have been fashionable at the court of King Charles II but were a little eccentric for Victorian taste.

At Oxford, Wilde became a follower of John Ruskin, a writer, poet and Oxford professor who was considered a leader of the Aesthetic Movement in Britain. The Aesthetic Movement consisted of artists, art lovers, and thinkers who loved art for its own sake – they believed it existed for no other reason than to bring pleasure and enlightenment.

Many Aesthetics were regarded as being hedonists – that pleasure was life's ultimate goal. Coupled with Wilde's lack of religious beliefs, his leaning towards Aestheticism and hedonism made him unpopular with his more conventional contemporaries. At Oxford he became a protégé of Walter Pater, a writer and essayist who championed hedonism.

While still a student at Oxford, Wilde toured northern Italy. He was typical enough of his class – the European tour was considered a necessary part of a gentleman's education. Oscar began writing poetry, inspired by Italy. In 1878 he was awarded the Newdigate prize for his poem "Ravenna".

The Newdigate Prize had been established in 1805 in memory of Sir Roger Newdigate and was awarded to a student for the best poem up to three hundred lines. Oxford published "Ravenna" in a paperback edition – it was Wilde's first published book. Oscar was asked how he envisioned his life after Oxford and in part he prophetically replied "Somehow or other I'll be famous, and if not famous, I'll be notorious."

Wilde's father Sir William died while his son was attending Oxford. One of Oscar's illegitimate half-brothers, Henry, took over the support of the family for a short time. Somehow Oscar was able to pursue his studies though the family was strapped for funds. Wilde earned his Bachelor of Arts degree from Oxford, graduating with honors in 1878. It was time to move on again – to London.

Adulthood of Oscar Wilde

Oscar Wilde finished his degree at Oxford in 1878 and moved to London the next year. His goal to achieve fame, or notoriety, had begun. His lifestyle was flamboyant and theatrical. Oscar used theatre costumers to create his wardrobe, rather than conventional tailors.

Oscar became known for the sunflowers and lilies he sported in his buttonholes. Wilde was joining his mother in London as well – after the death of her husband Sir William, she established a salon in Chelsea, the same district of the city that Oscar was to live in for many years.

Wilde had not been a stranger to relationships with men prior to graduating from Oxford. He also had relationships with women – some have described Oscar as homosexual, but others believe he was bisexual. While briefly in Ireland after leaving Oxford he courted Florence Balcombe.

Florence, a native of Dublin, was considered a beauty. She turned down Oscar's proposal of marriage and soon married Bram Stoker, the author of *Dracula*. Stoker had been a friend and supporter of Wilde's and after a cool period, their friendship resumed.

Wilde soon had a collection of poetry, *Poems*, published within a couple of years of his arrival in London. Many of the poems had been previously published in Irish periodicals. In 1881, he was living in South Chelsea, as a boarder in an artist's household, and in the census of that year was listed as "literature, author".

His painter landlord and friend, Frank Miles, was later represented in his only novel, *The Picture of Dorian Gray.* Apparently Frank and Oscar were strapped for cash, and had just moved there from more luxurious digs in Bloomsbury Square. However, they were hardly living in poverty, as this neighborhood in Chelsea was populated by middle class people.

Wilde's book of poetry was marginally better received in America than it was in Britain. *Punch* magazine criticized him for being unoriginal. The Oxford Debating Society refused a gift copy of *Poems*, saying the "father" of the verses was not Wilde at all, but Shakespeare, Donne, Lord Byron, and others.

Wilde did receive some acclaim and publicity for his poetry and embarked upon a lecture tour of North America in 1882. During that tour he met Henry Wadsworth Longfellow, Oliver Wendell Holmes, and Walt Whitman. Overall, though, the average American found him too much of a dandy and did not appreciate Aestheticism. One clothing manufacturer used a cartoonish figure of the writer in an advertisement – calling him "Wild Oscar". While American men found him ridiculous, American women apparently loved his style.

The 1880's were a busy decade for Oscar Wilde. In 1881 he worked as an art reviewer and briefly lived in Paris in 1883. He gave lectures all over Britain in 1883 and 1884 as he had grown weary of the London scene. He took a stab at being conventional and respectable – on May 29th, 1884 he married Constance Mary Lloyd, who was the daughter of a prominent Irish barrister, Horace Lloyd. He called himself a "gentleman" on the marriage certificate and his address was the fashionable and expensive Grosvenor Square.

Their wedding was a staged affair – typical of Oscar's theatricality. The couple honeymooned in Paris and returned to their home on Tite Street, Chelsea. Oscar and Constance had two sons, Cyril and Vyvyan, within a few years of marriage. Wilde's reasons for marrying remain something of a mystery. His sexual orientation may indeed have been bisexual, or he may sincerely have wanted to be seen as more respectable. He may have wrestled with his conscience about his lifestyle.

Apparently Constance, like many wives of brilliant artists, faded in comparison to her flamboyant husband. She was attractive but could not hope to compete with him on an intellectual and creative level. A brilliant wife may have challenged Oscar, but Constance offered no such brilliance, although she did bring a dowry to the marriage which was spent on remodelling their house in Chelsea. The couple dealt with a shortage of ready cash throughout their marriage.

Taking on the role of husband and father, Wilde sought work in his field to help support his growing family. He worked as a drama critic and a book reviewer. Oscar became the editor of *Woman's World*, a respected magazine, from 1887-89. He also penned a column for the publication. In 1888 he published *The Happy Prince and Other Tales*. This was a collection of fairy and Irish folklore tales he had written for his children.

Oscar's stab at the conventional and respectable life seems to have lost its appeal within a few years. In 1886, possibly before or soon after the birth of his second son, he turned to the London gay scene where he met other homosexuals and male prostitutes. Soon he was often absent from home, having affairs with other men and drinking excessively.

His affair with a valet, Charles Parker, would come back to haunt him when Parker testified as a prosecution witness at Wilde's trial in 1895. It was not long before Oscar met Lord Alfred Douglas, with whom he embarked upon a relationship that would be Wilde's downfall. During this period Oscar Wilde was at his most creative and most famous works were produced then.

Wilde separated from Constance in 1895. As well as letting his marriage slip away, Wilde also gave up his editorship at *Woman's World* and began devoting his writing hours to essays on the Aesthetic outlook – art for art's sake. It seems apparent at this time that he had grown tired of his brief flirtation with convention and turned to a more hedonistic lifestyle that suited him better.

The Picture of Dorian Gray was published in 1890. The book's ultimate message is that sin is punished. While Dorian lives the life of eternal youth, his portrait ages and reflects all of his misdeeds and crimes, including the murder of his portrait painter, who represents his conscience. Of all of Wilde's works, his only novel is the one best known to the general public and was even made into a Hollywood movie in 1945, long after the author's death.

The public's reaction to *Dorian Gray*, which was first published in a serialized form in *Lippincott's Magazine*, was predictably one of shock and discomfort. The homoeroticism of the novel was evident and this was not something the average Victorian had much exposure to. Hypocrisy reared its ugly head – while some members of "society" were titillated and entertained by its homosexual members, they did not want to be seen to support homosexuality as a lifestyle.

The prevailing Victorians, whose values centered on family, church, and a structured class system found anything it viewed as deviant hard to come to terms with. The fact also remained that homosexual practices were illegal. The homosexual element aside, many readers and even literary critics were at a loss to understand what the book was about.

The years 1891 to 1895 were productive years for Oscar Wilde. As well as having *The Picture of Dorian Gray* published in book form in 1891, Wilde also published *A House of Pomegranates*, *Lord Arthur Savile's Crime*, and *Intentions*. Despite the uproar over *Dorian Gray*, Wilde achieved much acclaim and the notoriety that followed him did not seem to hurt his career in the years that followed its debut.

In 1892, Oscar's first successful play, *Lady Windermere's Fan,* was presented to the public at St. James Theatre in London. It was a huge success and received glowing reviews. Immediately after this, Wilde went to Paris, where he wrote *Salome*. This play was written as a vehicle for the actress Sarah Bernhardt in the lead role. Unfortunately it was not presented in England, as there was an old law that prohibited Biblical characters was being portrayed on stage. The play was published in written form in both France and Britain.

Around the same time, Wilde announced that he was giving up his British citizenship to become French. As events would transpire, he did not make steps to complete the process and within a few years he was on trial in England for his homosexual activities.

In 1893 Wilde saw more creative success with the production of and acclaim for *A Woman of No Importance*, which dealt with the subject of illegitimacy. Oscar must have tapped into his own family's experience of illegitimacy with the open acknowledgement of his half-siblings, fathered by Sir William Wilde.

1893 also saw the publication in book form of his poem *The Sphinx*. The next year Oscar produced his last plays – *The Importance of Being Earnest* and *An Ideal Husband*. It was said that Wilde was much more interested in talking, narrating, and having witty conversation than he was in writing. The writing of plays must have come much more naturally to him than writing novels.

His last plays enjoyed enormous success. *An Ideal Husband* was written and produced first but it was still running in London when *The Importance of Being Earnest* hit the stage as well. *The Importance of Being Earnest* was at the same time staged in New York. *An Ideal Husband* was seen by the Prince of Wales and congratulated the playwright personally.

Oscar Wilde had arrived – his lifelong creative brilliance was now enjoyed by a wider world. The theatre-going public was putting aside its distaste of homosexuality and many were accepting him as a fashionable addition to "society".

Wilde left London when *Earnest* went into rehearsal, and visited Algiers. His overwhelming success at home encouraged him to begin several new plays. Unfortunately the plays were never completed, as the writer had now to face the courts.

While Oscar Wilde had many fans, the Marquess of Queensberry was not among them. Queensberry, a Scottish lord by the name of John Sholto Douglas, had drawn up the modern rules for the sport of boxing, and was the father of Oscar's lover, Lord Alfred Bruce Douglas (known as "Bosie"). Douglas was a handsome young man who came under Wilde's spell in the early 1890's.

The two had several photographic portraits taken in which Alfred looks very young, being in his early twenties. Although Oscar was older and accomplished, it seems to have been Douglas who introduced him to the underworld of male prostitution. While Wilde certainly had a number of relationships with men that were not entirely sexual, a part of his life now was given over to dangerous liaisons with anonymous male prostitutes.

Oscar must have known this behavior might come back to haunt him – he was now a public person and it would only be a matter of time until a scandal blew wide open.

Bosie's father was not happy with the intimate relationship his son was engaged in with Wilde. He left Wilde a card at his club in which he accused the writer as "posing" as a homosexual (the Marquess used the term "Sodomite") and Oscar decided to take Queensberry to court for libel.

Officially asked if he was a homosexual, Wilde denied it. He then went to Monte Carlo with Douglas, and the young lord's father set about collecting the evidence he needed to support his claim that Wilde was gay. He employed Oscar's old rival from Trinity College to collect evidence on the writer's sexual habits.

The Marquess won his case, proving to the satisfaction of the courts that Wilde was practicing homosexual. Oscar was not allowed bail and was not allowed to prepare a defence for himself when the charge came to trial. The Marquess claimed all of Wilde's assets, including his house on Tite Street, Chelsea. The author, languishing in jail, was now bankrupt.

Wilde's first trial resulted in a hung jury. Alfred Douglas, now cut off from his family, paid Oscar's bail. A few weeks later his second trial resulted in Oscar being found guilty. One of the pieces of evidence was a letter Oscar had written to Alfred – while not lurid, it certainly speaks of a relationship of love and passion.

Wilde was sentenced to two years old hard labor – and the judge admonished him for indulging in acts that were worse than rape or murder. Alfred Douglas himself was not charged with anything – he was seen as the sinned against party and undoubtedly his father's influence helped.

For most of his time in jail, Wilde had no access to writing implements or material. Towards the end he was and that is when he wrote the moving *De Profundis* in which he described his impressions of his incarceration, particularly his state of mind. A moving piece, it includes the observation: "It is always twilight in one's cell, as it is always twilight in one's heart".

Wilde was released from jail in May 1897 and he left immediately for France, never setting foot in Britain again. He lived in France with two old friends, using a pseudonym. Oscar blamed the two Douglases for involving him in their family squabble – he was their victim, caught between a father and son.

Oscar Wilde wrote one more published item before he died – *The Ballad of Reading Gaol.* He did see Alfred Douglas again, and they traveled together to Italy. Surprisingly, Constance Wilde joined her husband in Italy. Oscar wanted to reconcile with her and mend their marriage. She refused, as he could give her no assurances that his affair with Douglas would end.

Wilde never saw his young sons after 1895. Their mother changed their surname to Holland, a name from her side of the family. The boys were sent abroad. The elder son, Cyril, died during WWI. The younger son, Vyvyan, also served during WWI but survived to become a writer and was given the Order of the British Empire. His son Merlin Holland, still living as of 2011, is a Wilde biographer.

Constance Lloyd Wilde died in 1898 – she and Oscar never did reconcile. Alfred Douglas lived until he was almost 75, dying in 1940. He is now considered a very accomplished poet and sonnet writer, one of the best of his time.

Wilde died on November 30th, 1900, only three and a half years after his release from jail. He died of cerebral meningitis. As he lay dying, he was baptised a Roman Catholic.

Oscar Wilde is regarded more today for his celebrated notoriety and his imprisonment for homosexual practices. However, his brilliance has not been diminished, for he was not simply part of a celebrity scandal, but a clever and fascinating writer whose works live on.

Play: The Importance of Being Earnest

A Trivial Comedy for Serious People

By Oscar Wilde

Characters

John Worthing, J.P.

Algernon Moncrieff

Rev. Canon Chasuble, D.D.

Merriman, Butler

Lane, Manservant

Lady Bracknell

Hon. Gwendolen Fairfax

Cecily Cardew

Miss Prism, Governess

TIME: The Present.

First Act

SCENE

Morning-room in Algernon's flat in Half-Moon Street. The room is luxuriously and artistically furnished. The sound of a piano is heard in the adjoining room.

[Lane is arranging afternoon tea on the table, and after the music has ceased, Algernon enters.]

Algernon. Did you hear what I was playing, Lane?

Lane. I didn't think it polite to listen, sir.

Algernon. I'm sorry for that, for your sake. I don't play accurately--any one can play accurately--but I play with wonderful expression. As far as the piano is concerned, sentiment is my forte. I keep science for Life.

Lane. Yes, sir.

Algernon. And, speaking of the science of Life, have you got the cucumber sandwiches cut for Lady Bracknell?

Lane. Yes, sir. [Hands them on a salver.]

Algernon. [Inspects them, takes two, and sits down on the sofa.] Oh! . . . by the way, Lane, I see from your book that on Thursday night, when Lord Shoreman and Mr. Worthing were dining with me, eight bottles of champagne are entered as having been consumed.

Lane. Yes, sir; eight bottles and a pint.

Algernon. Why is it that at a bachelor's establishment the servants invariably drink the champagne? I ask merely for information.

Lane. I attribute it to the superior quality of the wine, sir. I have often observed that in married households the champagne is rarely of a first-rate brand.

Algernon. Good heavens! Is marriage so demoralising as that?

Lane. I believe it *is* a very pleasant state, sir. I have had very little experience of it myself up to the present. I have only been married once. That was in consequence of a misunderstanding between myself and a young person.

Algernon. [Languidly.] I don't know that I am much interested in your family life, Lane.

Lane. No, sir; it is not a very interesting subject. I never think of it myself.

Algernon. Very natural, I am sure. That will do, Lane, thank you.

Lane. Thank you, sir. [Lane goes out.]

Algernon. Lane's views on marriage seem somewhat lax. Really, if the lower orders don't set us a good example, what on earth is the use of them? They seem, as a class, to have absolutely no sense of moral responsibility.

[Enter Lane.]

Lane. Mr. Ernest Worthing.

[Enter Jack.]

[Lane goes out.]

Algernon. How are you, my dear Ernest? What brings you up to town?

Jack. Oh, pleasure, pleasure! What else should bring one anywhere? Eating as usual, I see, Algy!

Algernon. [Stiffly.] I believe it is customary in good society to take some slight refreshment at five o'clock. Where have you been since last Thursday?

Jack. [Sitting down on the sofa.] In the country.

Algernon. What on earth do you do there?

Jack. [Pulling off his gloves.] When one is in town one amuses oneself. When one is in the country one amuses other people. It is excessively boring.

Algernon. And who are the people you amuse?

Jack. [Airily.] Oh, neighbours, neighbours.

Algernon. Got nice neighbours in your part of Shropshire?

Jack. Perfectly horrid! Never speak to one of them.

Algernon. How immensely you must amuse them! [Goes over and takes sandwich.] By the way, Shropshire is your county, is it not?

Jack. Eh? Shropshire? Yes, of course. Hallo! Why all these cups? Why cucumber sandwiches? Why such reckless extravagance in one so young? Who is coming to tea?

Algernon. Oh! merely Aunt Augusta and Gwendolen.

Jack. How perfectly delightful!

Algernon. Yes, that is all very well; but I am afraid Aunt Augusta won't quite approve of your being here.

Jack. May I ask why?

Algernon. My dear fellow, the way you flirt with Gwendolen is perfectly disgraceful. It is almost as bad as the way Gwendolen flirts with you.

Jack. I am in love with Gwendolen. I have come up to town expressly to propose to her.

Algernon. I thought you had come up for pleasure? . . . I call that business.

Jack. How utterly unromantic you are!

Algernon. I really don't see anything romantic in proposing. It is very romantic to be in love. But there is nothing romantic about a definite proposal. Why, one may be accepted. One usually is, I believe. Then the excitement is all over. The very essence of romance is uncertainty. If ever I get married, I'll certainly try to forget the fact.

Jack. I have no doubt about that, dear Algy. The Divorce Court was specially invented for people whose memories are so curiously constituted.

Algernon. Oh! there is no use speculating on that subject. Divorces are made in Heaven--[Jack puts out his hand to take a sandwich. Algernon at once interferes.] Please don't touch the cucumber sandwiches. They are ordered specially for Aunt Augusta. [Takes one and eats it.]

Jack. Well, you have been eating them all the time.

Algernon. That is quite a different matter. She is my aunt. [Takes plate from below.] Have some bread and butter. The bread and butter is for Gwendolen. Gwendolen is devoted to bread and butter.

Jack. [Advancing to table and helping himself.] And very good bread and butter it is too.

Algernon. Well, my dear fellow, you need not eat as if you were going to eat it all. You behave as if you were married to her already. You are not married to her already, and I don't think you ever will be.

Jack. Why on earth do you say that?

Algernon. Well, in the first place girls never marry the men they flirt with. Girls don't think it right.

Jack. Oh, that is nonsense!

Algernon. It isn't. It is a great truth. It accounts for the extraordinary number of bachelors that one sees all over the place. In the second place, I don't give my consent.

Jack. Your consent!

Algernon. My dear fellow, Gwendolen is my first cousin. And before I allow you to marry her, you will have to clear up the whole question of Cecily. [Rings bell.]

Jack. Cecily! What on earth do you mean? What do you mean, Algy, by Cecily! I don't know any one of the name of Cecily.

[Enter Lane.]

Algernon. Bring me that cigarette case Mr. Worthing left in the smoking- room the last time he dined here.

Lane. Yes, sir. [Lane goes out.]

Jack. Do you mean to say you have had my cigarette case all this time? I wish to goodness you had let me know. I have been writing frantic letters to Scotland Yard about it. I was very nearly offering a large reward.

Algernon. Well, I wish you would offer one. I happen to be more than usually hard up.

Jack. There is no good offering a large reward now that the thing is found.

[Enter Lane with the cigarette case on a salver. Algernon takes it at once. Lane goes out.]

Algernon. I think that is rather mean of you, Ernest, I must say. [Opens case and examines it.] However, it makes no matter, for, now that I look at the inscription inside, I find that the thing isn't yours after all.

Jack. Of course it's mine. [Moving to him.] You have seen me with it a hundred times, and you have no right whatsoever to read what is written inside. It is a very ungentlemanly thing to read a private cigarette case.

Algernon. Oh! it is absurd to have a hard and fast rule about what one should read and what one shouldn't. More than half of modern culture depends on what one shouldn't read.

Jack. I am quite aware of the fact, and I don't propose to discuss modern culture. It isn't the sort of thing one should talk of in private. I simply want my cigarette case back.

Algernon. Yes; but this isn't your cigarette case. This cigarette case is a present from some one of the name of Cecily, and you said you didn't know any one of that name.

Jack. Well, if you want to know, Cecily happens to be my aunt.

Algernon. Your aunt!

Jack. Yes. Charming old lady she is, too. Lives at Tunbridge Wells. Just give it back to me, Algy.

Algernon. [Retreating to back of sofa.] But why does she call herself little Cecily if she is your aunt and lives at Tunbridge Wells? [Reading.] 'From little Cecily with her fondest love.'

Jack. [Moving to sofa and kneeling upon it.] My dear fellow, what on earth is there in that? Some aunts are tall, some aunts are not tall. That is a matter that surely an aunt may be allowed to decide for herself. You seem to think that every aunt should be exactly like your aunt! That is absurd! For Heaven's sake give me back my cigarette case. [Follows Algernon round the room.]

Algernon. Yes. But why does your aunt call you her uncle? 'From little Cecily, with her fondest love to her dear Uncle Jack.' There is no objection, I admit, to an aunt being a small aunt, but why an aunt, no matter what her size may be, should call her own nephew her uncle, I can't quite make out. Besides, your name isn't Jack at all; it is Ernest.

Jack. It isn't Ernest; it's Jack.

Algernon. You have always told me it was Ernest. I have introduced you to every one as Ernest. You answer to the name of Ernest. You look as if your name was Ernest. You are the most earnest-looking person I ever saw in my life. It is perfectly absurd your saying that your name isn't Ernest. It's on your cards. Here is one of them. [Taking it from case.] 'Mr. Ernest Worthing, B. 4, The Albany.' I'll keep this as a proof that your name is Ernest if ever you attempt to deny it to me, or to Gwendolen, or to any one else. [Puts the card in his pocket.]

Jack. Well, my name is Ernest in town and Jack in the country, and the cigarette case was given to me in the country.

Algernon. Yes, but that does not account for the fact that your small Aunt Cecily, who lives at Tunbridge Wells, calls you her dear uncle. Come, old boy, you had much better have the thing out at once.

Jack. My dear Algy, you talk exactly as if you were a dentist. It is very vulgar to talk like a dentist when one isn't a dentist. It produces a false impression.

Algernon. Well, that is exactly what dentists always do. Now, go on! Tell me the whole thing. I may mention that I have always suspected you of being a confirmed and secret Bunburyist; and I am quite sure of it now.

Jack. Bunburyist? What on earth do you mean by a Bunburyist?

Algernon. I'll reveal to you the meaning of that incomparable expression as soon as you are kind enough to inform me why you are Ernest in town and Jack in the country.

Jack. Well, produce my cigarette case first.

Algernon. Here it is. [Hands cigarette case.] Now produce your explanation, and pray make it improbable. [Sits on sofa.]

Jack. My dear fellow, there is nothing improbable about my explanation at all. In fact it's perfectly ordinary. Old Mr. Thomas Cardew, who adopted me when I was a little boy, made me in his will guardian to his grand-daughter, Miss Cecily Cardew. Cecily, who addresses me as her uncle from motives of respect that you could not possibly appreciate, lives at my place in the country under the charge of her admirable governess, Miss Prism.

Algernon. Where is that place in the country, by the way?

Jack. That is nothing to you, dear boy. You are not going to be invited . . . I may tell you candidly that the place is not in Shropshire.

Algernon. I suspected that, my dear fellow! I have Bunburyed all over Shropshire on two separate occasions. Now, go on. Why are you Ernest in town and Jack in the country?

Jack. My dear Algy, I don't know whether you will be able to understand my real motives. You are hardly serious enough. When one is placed in the position of guardian, one has to adopt a very high moral tone on all subjects. It's one's duty to do so. And as a high moral tone can hardly be said to conduce very much to either one's health or one's happiness, in order to get up to town I have always pretended to have a younger brother of the name of Ernest, who lives in the Albany, and gets into the most dreadful scrapes. That, my dear Algy, is the whole truth pure and simple.

Algernon. The truth is rarely pure and never simple. Modern life would be very tedious if it were either, and modern literature a complete impossibility!

Jack. That wouldn't be at all a bad thing.

Algernon. Literary criticism is not your forte, my dear fellow. Don't try it. You should leave that to people who haven't been at a University. They do it so well in the daily papers. What you really are is a Bunburyist. I was quite right in saying you were a Bunburyist. You are one of the most advanced Bunburyists I know.

Jack. What on earth do you mean?

Algernon. You have invented a very useful younger brother called Ernest, in order that you may be able to come up to town as often as you like. I have invented an invaluable permanent invalid called Bunbury, in order that I may be able to go down into the country whenever I choose. Bunbury is perfectly invaluable. If it wasn't for Bunbury's extraordinary bad health, for instance, I wouldn't be able to dine with you at Willis's to- night, for I have been really engaged to Aunt Augusta for more than a week.

Jack. I haven't asked you to dine with me anywhere to-night.

Algernon. I know. You are absurdly careless about sending out invitations. It is very foolish of you. Nothing annoys people so much as not receiving invitations.

Jack. You had much better dine with your Aunt Augusta.

Algernon. I haven't the smallest intention of doing anything of the kind. To begin with, I dined there on Monday, and once a week is quite enough to dine with one's own relations. In the second place, whenever I do dine there I am always treated as a member of the family, and sent down with either no woman at all, or two. In the third place, I know perfectly well whom she will place me next to, to-night. She will place me next Mary Farquhar, who always flirts with her own husband across the dinner-table. That is not very pleasant. Indeed, it is not even decent . . . and that sort of thing is enormously on the increase. The amount of women in London who flirt with their own husbands is perfectly scandalous. It looks so bad. It is simply washing one's clean linen in public. Besides, now that I know you to be a confirmed Bunburyist I naturally want to talk to you about Bunburying. I want to tell you the rules.

Jack. I'm not a Bunburyist at all. If Gwendolen accepts me, I am going to kill my brother, indeed I think I'll kill him in any case. Cecily is a little too much interested in him. It is rather a bore. So I am going to get rid of Ernest. And I strongly advise you to do the same with Mr. . . . with your invalid friend who has the absurd name.

Algernon. Nothing will induce me to part with Bunbury, and if you ever get married, which seems to me extremely problematic, you will be very glad to know Bunbury. A man who marries without knowing Bunbury has a very tedious time of it.

Jack. That is nonsense. If I marry a charming girl like Gwendolen, and she is the only girl I ever saw in my life that I would marry, I certainly won't want to know Bunbury.

Algernon. Then your wife will. You don't seem to realise, that in married life three is company and two is none.

Jack. [Sententiously.] That, my dear young friend, is the theory that the corrupt French Drama has been propounding for the last fifty years.

Algernon. Yes; and that the happy English home has proved in half the time.

Jack. For heaven's sake, don't try to be cynical. It's perfectly easy to be cynical.

Algernon. My dear fellow, it isn't easy to be anything nowadays. There's such a lot of beastly competition about. [The sound of an electric bell is heard.] Ah! that must be Aunt Augusta. Only relatives, or creditors, ever ring in that Wagnerian manner. Now, if I get her out of the way for ten minutes, so that you can have an opportunity for proposing to Gwendolen, may I dine with you to-night at Willis's?

Jack. I suppose so, if you want to.

Algernon. Yes, but you must be serious about it. I hate people who are not serious about meals. It is so shallow of them.

[Enter Lane.]

Lane. Lady Bracknell and Miss Fairfax.

[Algernon goes forward to meet them. Enter Lady Bracknell and Gwendolen.]

Lady Bracknell. Good afternoon, dear Algernon, I hope you are behaving very well.

Algernon. I'm feeling very well, Aunt Augusta.

Lady Bracknell. That's not quite the same thing. In fact the two things rarely go together. [Sees Jack and bows to him with icy coldness.]

Algernon. [To Gwendolen.] Dear me, you are smart!

Gwendolen. I am always smart! Am I not, Mr. Worthing?

Jack. You're quite perfect, Miss Fairfax.

Gwendolen. Oh! I hope I am not that. It would leave no room for developments, and I intend to develop in many directions. [Gwendolen and Jack sit down together in the corner.]

Lady Bracknell. I'm sorry if we are a little late, Algernon, but I was obliged to call on dear Lady Harbury. I hadn't been there since her poor husband's death. I never saw a woman so altered; she looks quite twenty years younger. And now I'll have a cup of tea, and one of those nice cucumber sandwiches you promised me.

Algernon. Certainly, Aunt Augusta. [Goes over to tea-table.]

Lady Bracknell. Won't you come and sit here, Gwendolen?

Gwendolen. Thanks, mamma, I'm quite comfortable where I am.

Algernon. [Picking up empty plate in horror.] Good heavens! Lane! Why are there no cucumber sandwiches? I ordered them specially.

Lane. [Gravely.] There were no cucumbers in the market this morning, sir. I went down twice.

Algernon. No cucumbers!

Lane. No, sir. Not even for ready money.

Algernon. That will do, Lane, thank you.

Lane. Thank you, sir. [Goes out.]

Algernon. I am greatly distressed, Aunt Augusta, about there being no cucumbers, not even for ready money.

Lady Bracknell. It really makes no matter, Algernon. I had some crumpets with Lady Harbury, who seems to me to be living entirely for pleasure now.

Algernon. I hear her hair has turned quite gold from grief.

Lady Bracknell. It certainly has changed its colour. From what cause I, of course, cannot say. [Algernon crosses and hands tea.] Thank you. I've quite a treat for you to-night, Algernon. I am going to send you down with Mary Farquhar. She is such a nice woman, and so attentive to her husband. It's delightful to watch them.

Algernon. I am afraid, Aunt Augusta, I shall have to give up the pleasure of dining with you to-night after all.

Lady Bracknell. [Frowning.] I hope not, Algernon. It would put my table completely out. Your uncle would have to dine upstairs. Fortunately he is accustomed to that.

Algernon. It is a great bore, and, I need hardly say, a terrible disappointment to me, but the fact is I have just had a telegram to say that my poor friend Bunbury is very ill again. [Exchanges glances with Jack.] They seem to think I should be with him.

Lady Bracknell. It is very strange. This Mr. Bunbury seems to suffer from curiously bad health.

Algernon. Yes; poor Bunbury is a dreadful invalid.

Lady Bracknell. Well, I must say, Algernon, that I think it is high time that Mr. Bunbury made up his mind whether he was going to live or to die. This shilly-shallying with the question is absurd. Nor do I in any way approve of the modern sympathy with invalids. I consider it morbid. Illness of any kind is hardly a thing to be encouraged in others. Health is the primary duty of life. I am always telling that to your poor uncle, but he never seems to take much notice . . . as far as any improvement in his ailment goes. I should be much obliged if you would ask Mr. Bunbury, from me, to be kind enough not to have a relapse on Saturday, for I rely on you to arrange my music for me. It is my last reception, and one wants something that will encourage conversation, particularly at the end of the season when every one has practically said whatever they had to say, which, in most cases, was probably not much.

Algernon. I'll speak to Bunbury, Aunt Augusta, if he is still conscious, and I think I can promise you he'll be all right by Saturday. Of course the music is a great difficulty. You see, if one plays good music, people don't listen, and if one plays bad music people don't talk. But I'll run over the programme I've drawn out, if you will kindly come into the next room for a moment.

Lady Bracknell. Thank you, Algernon. It is very thoughtful of you. [Rising, and following Algernon.] I'm sure the programme will be delightful, after a few expurgations. French songs I cannot possibly allow. People always seem to think that they are improper, and either look shocked, which is vulgar, or laugh, which is worse. But German sounds a thoroughly respectable language, and indeed, I believe is so. Gwendolen, you will accompany me.

Gwendolen. Certainly, mamma.

[Lady Bracknell and Algernon go into the music-room, Gwendolen remains behind.]

Jack. Charming day it has been, Miss Fairfax.

Gwendolen. Pray don't talk to me about the weather, Mr. Worthing. Whenever people talk to me about the weather, I always feel quite certain that they mean something else. And that makes me so nervous.

Jack. I do mean something else.

Gwendolen. I thought so. In fact, I am never wrong.

Jack. And I would like to be allowed to take advantage of Lady Bracknell's temporary absence . . .

Gwendolen. I would certainly advise you to do so. Mamma has a way of coming back suddenly into a room that I have often had to speak to her about.

Jack. [Nervously.] Miss Fairfax, ever since I met you I have admired you more than any girl . . . I have ever met since . . . I met you.

Gwendolen. Yes, I am quite well aware of the fact. And I often wish that in public, at any rate, you had been more demonstrative. For me you have always had an irresistible fascination. Even before I met you I was far from indifferent to you. [Jack looks at her in amazement.] We live, as I hope you know, Mr. Worthing, in an age of ideals. The fact is constantly mentioned in the more expensive monthly magazines, and has reached the provincial pulpits, I am told; and my ideal has always been to love some one of the name of Ernest. There is something in that name that inspires absolute confidence. The moment Algernon first mentioned to me that he had a friend called Ernest, I knew I was destined to love you.

Jack. You really love me, Gwendolen?

Gwendolen. Passionately!

Jack. Darling! You don't know how happy you've made me.

Gwendolen. My own Ernest!

Jack. But you don't really mean to say that you couldn't love me if my name wasn't Ernest?

Gwendolen. But your name is Ernest.

Jack. Yes, I know it is. But supposing it was something else? Do you mean to say you couldn't love me then?

Gwendolen. [Glibly.] Ah! that is clearly a metaphysical speculation, and like most metaphysical speculations has very little reference at all to the actual facts of real life, as we know them.

Jack. Personally, darling, to speak quite candidly, I don't much care about the name of Ernest . . . I don't think the name suits me at all.

Gwendolen. It suits you perfectly. It is a divine name. It has a music of its own. It produces vibrations.

Jack. Well, really, Gwendolen, I must say that I think there are lots of other much nicer names. I think Jack, for instance, a charming name.

Gwendolen. Jack? . . . No, there is very little music in the name Jack, if any at all, indeed. It does not thrill. It produces absolutely no vibrations . . . I have known several Jacks, and they all, without exception, were more than usually plain. Besides, Jack is a notorious domesticity for John! And I pity any woman who is married to a man called John. She would probably never be allowed to know the entrancing pleasure of a single moment's solitude. The only really safe name is Ernest

Jack. Gwendolen, I must get christened at once--I mean we must get married at once. There is no time to be lost.

Gwendolen. Married, Mr. Worthing?

Jack. [Astounded.] Well . . . surely. You know that I love you, and you led me to believe, Miss Fairfax, that you were not absolutely indifferent to me.

Gwendolen. I adore you. But you haven't proposed to me yet. Nothing has been said at all about marriage. The subject has not even been touched on.

Jack. Well . . . may I propose to you now?

Gwendolen. I think it would be an admirable opportunity. And to spare you any possible disappointment, Mr. Worthing, I think it only fair to tell you quite frankly before-hand that I am fully determined to accept you.

Jack. Gwendolen!

Gwendolen. Yes, Mr. Worthing, what have you got to say to me?

Jack. You know what I have got to say to you.

Gwendolen. Yes, but you don't say it.

Jack. Gwendolen, will you marry me? [Goes on his knees.]

Gwendolen. Of course I will, darling. How long you have been about it! I am afraid you have had very little experience in how to propose.

Jack. My own one, I have never loved any one in the world but you.

Gwendolen. Yes, but men often propose for practice. I know my brother Gerald does. All my girl-friends tell me so. What wonderfully blue eyes you have, Ernest! They are quite, quite, blue. I hope you will always look at me just like that, especially when there are other people present. [Enter Lady Bracknell.]

Lady Bracknell. Mr. Worthing! Rise, sir, from this semi-recumbent posture. It is most indecorous.

Gwendolen. Mamma! [He tries to rise; she restrains him.] I must beg you to retire. This is no place for you. Besides, Mr. Worthing has not quite finished yet.

Lady Bracknell. Finished what, may I ask?

Gwendolen. I am engaged to Mr. Worthing, mamma. [They rise together.]

Lady Bracknell. Pardon me, you are not engaged to any one. When you do become engaged to some one, I, or your father, should his health permit him, will inform you of the fact. An engagement should come on a young girl as a surprise, pleasant or unpleasant, as the case may be. It is hardly a matter that she could be allowed to arrange for herself . . . And now I have a few questions to put to you, Mr. Worthing. While I am making these inquiries, you, Gwendolen, will wait for me below in the carriage.

Gwendolen. [Reproachfully.] Mamma!

Lady Bracknell. In the carriage, Gwendolen! [Gwendolen goes to the door. She and Jack blow kisses to each other behind Lady Bracknell's back. Lady Bracknell looks vaguely about as if she could not understand what the noise was. Finally turns round.] Gwendolen, the carriage!

Gwendolen. Yes, mamma. [Goes out, looking back at Jack.]

Lady Bracknell. [Sitting down.] You can take a seat, Mr. Worthing.

[Looks in her pocket for note-book and pencil.]

Jack. Thank you, Lady Bracknell, I prefer standing.

Lady Bracknell. [Pencil and note-book in hand.] I feel bound to tell you that you are not down on my list of eligible young men, although I have the same list as the dear Duchess of Bolton has. We work together, in fact. However, I am quite ready to enter your name, should your answers be what a really affectionate mother requires. Do you smoke?

Jack. Well, yes, I must admit I smoke.

Lady Bracknell. I am glad to hear it. A man should always have an occupation of some kind. There are far too many idle men in London as it is. How old are you?

Jack. Twenty-nine.

Lady Bracknell. A very good age to be married at. I have always been of opinion that a man who desires to get married should know either everything or nothing. Which do you know?

Jack. [After some hesitation.] I know nothing, Lady Bracknell.

Lady Bracknell. I am pleased to hear it. I do not approve of anything that tampers with natural ignorance. Ignorance is like a delicate exotic fruit; touch it and the bloom is gone. The whole theory of modern education is radically unsound. Fortunately in England, at any rate, education produces no effect whatsoever. If it did, it would prove a serious danger to the upper classes, and probably lead to acts of violence in Grosvenor Square. What is your income?

Jack. Between seven and eight thousand a year.

Lady Bracknell. [Makes a note in her book.] In land, or in investments?

Jack. In investments, chiefly.

Lady Bracknell. That is satisfactory. What between the duties expected of one during one's lifetime, and the duties exacted from one after one's death, land has ceased to be either a profit or a pleasure. It gives one position, and prevents one from keeping it up. That's all that can be said about land.

Jack. I have a country house with some land, of course, attached to it, about fifteen hundred acres, I believe; but I don't depend on that for my real income. In fact, as far as I can make out, the poachers are the only people who make anything out of it.

Lady Bracknell. A country house! How many bedrooms? Well, that point can be cleared up afterwards. You have a town house, I hope? A girl with a simple, unspoiled nature, like Gwendolen, could hardly be expected to reside in the country.

Jack. Well, I own a house in Belgrave Square, but it is let by the year to Lady Bloxham. Of course, I can get it back whenever I like, at six months' notice.

Lady Bracknell. Lady Bloxham? I don't know her.

Jack. Oh, she goes about very little. She is a lady considerably advanced in years.

Lady Bracknell. Ah, nowadays that is no guarantee of respectability of character. What number in Belgrave Square?

Jack. 149.

Lady Bracknell. [Shaking her head.] The unfashionable side. I thought there was something. However, that could easily be altered.

Jack. Do you mean the fashion, or the side?

Lady Bracknell. [Sternly.] Both, if necessary, I presume. What are your politics?

Jack. Well, I am afraid I really have none. I am a Liberal Unionist.

Lady Bracknell. Oh, they count as Tories. They dine with us. Or come in the evening, at any rate. Now to minor matters. Are your parents living?

Jack. I have lost both my parents.

Lady Bracknell. To lose one parent, Mr. Worthing, may be regarded as a misfortune; to lose both looks like carelessness. Who was your father? He was evidently a man of some wealth. Was he born in what the Radical papers call the purple of commerce, or did he rise from the ranks of the aristocracy?

Jack. I am afraid I really don't know. The fact is, Lady Bracknell, I said I had lost my parents. It would be nearer the truth to say that my parents seem to have lost me . . . I don't actually know who I am by birth. I was . . . well, I was found.

Lady Bracknell. Found!

Jack. The late Mr. Thomas Cardew, an old gentleman of a very charitable and kindly disposition, found me, and gave me the name of Worthing, because he happened to have a first-class ticket for Worthing in his pocket at the time. Worthing is a place in Sussex. It is a seaside resort.

Lady Bracknell. Where did the charitable gentleman who had a first-class ticket for this seaside resort find you?

Jack. [Gravely.] In a hand-bag.

Lady Bracknell. A hand-bag?

Jack. [Very seriously.] Yes, Lady Bracknell. I was in a hand-bag--a somewhat large, black leather hand-bag, with handles to it--an ordinary hand-bag in fact.

Lady Bracknell. In what locality did this Mr. James, or Thomas, Cardew come across this ordinary hand-bag?

Jack. In the cloak-room at Victoria Station. It was given to him in mistake for his own.

Lady Bracknell. The cloak-room at Victoria Station?

Jack. Yes. The Brighton line.

Lady Bracknell. The line is immaterial. Mr. Worthing, I confess I feel somewhat bewildered by what you have just told me. To be born, or at any rate bred, in a hand-bag, whether it had handles or not, seems to me to display a contempt for the ordinary decencies of family life that reminds one of the worst excesses of the French Revolution. And I presume you know what that unfortunate movement led to? As for the particular locality in which the hand-bag was found, a cloak-room at a railway station might serve to conceal a social indiscretion--has probably, indeed, been used for that purpose before now--but it could hardly be regarded as an assured basis for a recognised position in good society.

Jack. May I ask you then what you would advise me to do? I need hardly say I would do anything in the world to ensure Gwendolen's happiness.

Lady Bracknell. I would strongly advise you, Mr. Worthing, to try and acquire some relations as soon as possible, and to make a definite effort to produce at any rate one parent, of either sex, before the season is quite over.

Jack. Well, I don't see how I could possibly manage to do that. I can produce the hand-bag at any moment. It is in my dressing-room at home. I really think that should satisfy you, Lady Bracknell.

Lady Bracknell. Me, sir! What has it to do with me? You can hardly imagine that I and Lord Bracknell would dream of allowing our only daughter--a girl brought up with the utmost care--to marry into a cloak- room, and form an alliance with a parcel? Good morning, Mr. Worthing!

[Lady Bracknell sweeps out in majestic indignation.]

Jack. Good morning! [Algernon, from the other room, strikes up the Wedding March. Jack looks perfectly furious, and goes to the door.] For goodness' sake don't play that ghastly tune, Algy. How idiotic you are!

[The music stops and Algernon enters cheerily.]

Algernon. Didn't it go off all right, old boy? You don't mean to say Gwendolen refused you? I know it is a way she has. She is always refusing people. I think it is most ill-natured of her.

Jack. Oh, Gwendolen is as right as a trivet. As far as she is concerned, we are engaged. Her mother is perfectly unbearable. Never met such a Gorgon . . . I don't really know what a Gorgon is like, but I am quite sure that Lady Bracknell is one. In any case, she is a monster, without being a myth, which is rather unfair . . . I beg your pardon, Algy, I suppose I shouldn't talk about your own aunt in that way before you.

Algernon. My dear boy, I love hearing my relations abused. It is the only thing that makes me put up with them at all. Relations are simply a tedious pack of people, who haven't got the remotest knowledge of how to live, nor the smallest instinct about when to die.

Jack. Oh, that is nonsense!

Algernon. It isn't!

Jack. Well, I won't argue about the matter. You always want to argue about things.

Algernon. That is exactly what things were originally made for.

Jack. Upon my word, if I thought that, I'd shoot myself . . . [A pause.] You don't think there is any chance of Gwendolen becoming like her mother in about a hundred and fifty years, do you, Algy?

Algernon. All women become like their mothers. That is their tragedy. No man does. That's his.

Jack. Is that clever?

Algernon. It is perfectly phrased! and quite as true as any observation in civilised life should be.

Jack. I am sick to death of cleverness. Everybody is clever nowadays. You can't go anywhere without meeting clever people. The thing has become an absolute public nuisance. I wish to goodness we had a few fools left.

Algernon. We have.

Jack. I should extremely like to meet them. What do they talk about?

Algernon. The fools? Oh! about the clever people, of course.

Jack. What fools!

Algernon. By the way, did you tell Gwendolen the truth about your being Ernest in town, and Jack in the country?

Jack. [In a very patronising manner.] My dear fellow, the truth isn't quite the sort of thing one tells to a nice, sweet, refined girl. What extraordinary ideas you have about the way to behave to a woman!

Algernon. The only way to behave to a woman is to make love to her, if she is pretty, and to some one else, if she is plain.

Jack. Oh, that is nonsense.

Algernon. What about your brother? What about the profligate Ernest?

Jack. Oh, before the end of the week I shall have got rid of him. I'll say he died in Paris of apoplexy. Lots of people die of apoplexy, quite suddenly, don't they?

Algernon. Yes, but it's hereditary, my dear fellow. It's a sort of thing that runs in families. You had much better say a severe chill.

Jack. You are sure a severe chill isn't hereditary, or anything of that kind?

Algernon. Of course it isn't!

Jack. Very well, then. My poor brother Ernest to carried off suddenly, in Paris, by a severe chill. That gets rid of him.

Algernon. But I thought you said that . . . Miss Cardew was a little too much interested in your poor brother Ernest? Won't she feel his loss a good deal?

Jack. Oh, that is all right. Cecily is not a silly romantic girl, I am glad to say. She has got a capital appetite, goes long walks, and pays no attention at all to her lessons.

Algernon. I would rather like to see Cecily.

Jack. I will take very good care you never do. She is excessively pretty, and she is only just eighteen.

Algernon. Have you told Gwendolen yet that you have an excessively pretty ward who is only just eighteen?

Jack. Oh! one doesn't blurt these things out to people. Cecily and Gwendolen are perfectly certain to be extremely great friends. I'll bet you anything you like that half an hour after they have met, they will be calling each other sister.

Algernon. Women only do that when they have called each other a lot of other things first. Now, my dear boy, if we want to get a good table at Willis's, we really must go and dress. Do you know it is nearly seven?

Jack. [Irritably.] Oh! It always is nearly seven.

Algernon. Well, I'm hungry.

Jack. I never knew you when you weren't . . .

Algernon. What shall we do after dinner? Go to a theatre?

Jack. Oh no! I loathe listening.

Algernon. Well, let us go to the Club?

Jack. Oh, no! I hate talking.

Algernon. Well, we might trot round to the Empire at ten?

Jack. Oh, no! I can't bear looking at things. It is so silly.

Algernon. Well, what shall we do?

Jack. Nothing!

Algernon. It is awfully hard work doing nothing. However, I don't mind hard work where there is no definite object of any kind.

[Enter Lane.]

Lane. Miss Fairfax.

[Enter Gwendolen. Lane goes out.]

Algernon. Gwendolen, upon my word!

Gwendolen. Algy, kindly turn your back. I have something very particular to say to Mr. Worthing.

Algernon. Really, Gwendolen, I don't think I can allow this at all.

Gwendolen. Algy, you always adopt a strictly immoral attitude towards life. You are not quite old enough to do that. [Algernon retires to the fireplace.]

Jack. My own darling!

Gwendolen. Ernest, we may never be married. From the expression on mamma's face I fear we never shall. Few parents nowadays pay any regard to what their children say to them. The old-fashioned respect for the young is fast dying out. Whatever influence I ever had over mamma, I lost at the age of three. But although she may prevent us from becoming man and wife, and I may marry some one else, and marry often, nothing that she can possibly do can alter my eternal devotion to you.

Jack. Dear Gwendolen!

Gwendolen. The story of your romantic origin, as related to me by mamma, with unpleasing comments, has naturally stirred the deeper fibres of my nature. Your Christian name has an irresistible fascination. The simplicity of your character makes you exquisitely incomprehensible to me. Your town address at the Albany I have. What is your address in the country?

Jack. The Manor House, Woolton, Hertfordshire.

[Algernon, who has been carefully listening, smiles to himself, and writes the address on his shirt-cuff. Then picks up the Railway Guide.]

Gwendolen. There is a good postal service, I suppose? It may be necessary to do something desperate. That of course will require serious consideration. I will communicate with you daily.

Jack. My own one!

Gwendolen. How long do you remain in town?

Jack. Till Monday.

Gwendolen. Good! Algy, you may turn round now.

Algernon. Thanks, I've turned round already.

Gwendolen. You may also ring the bell.

Jack. You will let me see you to your carriage, my own darling?

Gwendolen. Certainly.

Jack. [To Lane, who now enters.] I will see Miss Fairfax out.

Lane. Yes, sir. [Jack and Gwendolen go off.]

[Lane presents several letters on a salver to Algernon. It is to be surmised that they are bills, as Algernon, after looking at the envelopes, tears them up.]

Algernon. A glass of sherry, Lane.

Lane. Yes, sir.

Algernon. To-morrow, Lane, I'm going Bunburying.

Lane. Yes, sir.

Algernon. I shall probably not be back till Monday. You can put up my dress clothes, my smoking jacket, and all the Bunbury suits . . .

Lane. Yes, sir. [Handing sherry.]

Algernon. I hope to-morrow will be a fine day, Lane.

Lane. It never is, sir.

Algernon. Lane, you're a perfect pessimist.

Lane. I do my best to give satisfaction, sir.

[Enter Jack. Lane goes off.]

Jack. There's a sensible, intellectual girl! the only girl I ever cared for in my life. [Algernon is laughing immoderately.] What on earth are you so amused at?

Algernon. Oh, I'm a little anxious about poor Bunbury, that is all.

Jack. If you don't take care, your friend Bunbury will get you into a serious scrape some day.

Algernon. I love scrapes. They are the only things that are never serious.

Jack. Oh, that's nonsense, Algy. You never talk anything but nonsense.

Algernon. Nobody ever does.

[Jack looks indignantly at him, and leaves the room. Algernon lights a cigarette, reads his shirt-cuff, and smiles.]

ACT DROP

Second Act

SCENE

Garden at the Manor House. A flight of grey stone steps leads up to the house. The garden, an old-fashioned one, full of roses. Time of year, July. Basket chairs, and a table covered with books, are set under a large yew-tree.

[Miss Prism discovered seated at the table. Cecily is at the back watering flowers.]

Miss Prism. [Calling.] Cecily, Cecily! Surely such a utilitarian occupation as the watering of flowers is rather Moulton's duty than yours? Especially at a moment when intellectual pleasures await you. Your German grammar is on the table. Pray open it at page fifteen. We will repeat yesterday's lesson.

Cecily. [Coming over very slowly.] But I don't like German. It isn't at all a becoming language. I know perfectly well that I look quite plain after my German lesson.

Miss Prism. Child, you know how anxious your guardian is that you should improve yourself in every way. He laid particular stress on your German, as he was leaving for town yesterday. Indeed, he always lays stress on your German when he is leaving for town.

Cecily. Dear Uncle Jack is so very serious! Sometimes he is so serious that I think he cannot be quite well.

Miss Prism. [Drawing herself up.] Your guardian enjoys the best of health, and his gravity of demeanour is especially to be commended in one so comparatively young as he is. I know no one who has a higher sense of duty and responsibility.

Cecily. I suppose that is why he often looks a little bored when we three are together.

Miss Prism. Cecily! I am surprised at you. Mr. Worthing has many troubles in his life. Idle merriment and triviality would be out of place in his conversation. You must remember his constant anxiety about that unfortunate young man his brother.

Cecily. I wish Uncle Jack would allow that unfortunate young man, his brother, to come down here sometimes. We might have a good influence over him, Miss Prism. I am sure you certainly would. You know German, and geology, and things of that kind influence a man very much. [Cecily begins to write in her diary.]

Miss Prism. [Shaking her head.] I do not think that even I could produce any effect on a character that according to his own brother's admission is irretrievably weak and vacillating. Indeed I am not sure that I would desire to reclaim him. I am not in favour of this modern mania for turning bad people into good people at a moment's notice. As a man sows so let him reap. You must put away your diary, Cecily. I really don't see why you should keep a diary at all.

Cecily. I keep a diary in order to enter the wonderful secrets of my life. If I didn't write them down, I should probably forget all about them.

Miss Prism. Memory, my dear Cecily, is the diary that we all carry about with us.

Cecily. Yes, but it usually chronicles the things that have never happened, and couldn't possibly have happened. I believe that Memory is responsible for nearly all the three-volume novels that Mudie sends us.

Miss Prism. Do not speak slightingly of the three-volume novel, Cecily. I wrote one myself in earlier days.

Cecily. Did you really, Miss Prism? How wonderfully clever you are! I hope it did not end happily? I don't like novels that end happily. They depress me so much.

Miss Prism. The good ended happily, and the bad unhappily. That is what Fiction means.

Cecily. I suppose so. But it seems very unfair. And was your novel ever published?

Miss Prism. Alas! no. The manuscript unfortunately was abandoned. [Cecily starts.] I use the word in the sense of lost or mislaid. To your work, child, these speculations are profitless.

Cecily. [Smiling.] But I see dear Dr. Chasuble coming up through the garden.

Miss Prism. [Rising and advancing.] Dr. Chasuble! This is indeed a pleasure.

[Enter Canon Chasuble.]

Chasuble. And how are we this morning? Miss Prism, you are, I trust, well?

Cecily. Miss Prism has just been complaining of a slight headache. I think it would do her so much good to have a short stroll with you in the Park, Dr. Chasuble.

Miss Prism. Cecily, I have not mentioned anything about a headache.

Cecily. No, dear Miss Prism, I know that, but I felt instinctively that you had a headache. Indeed I was thinking about that, and not about my German lesson, when the Rector came in.

Chasuble. I hope, Cecily, you are not inattentive.

Cecily. Oh, I am afraid I am.

Chasuble. That is strange. Were I fortunate enough to be Miss Prism's pupil, I would hang upon her lips. [Miss Prism glares.] I spoke metaphorically.--My metaphor was drawn from bees. Ahem! Mr. Worthing, I suppose, has not returned from town yet?

Miss Prism. We do not expect him till Monday afternoon.

Chasuble. Ah yes, he usually likes to spend his Sunday in London. He is not one of those whose sole aim is enjoyment, as, by all accounts, that unfortunate young man his brother seems to be. But I must not disturb Egeria and her pupil any longer.

Miss Prism. Egeria? My name is Laetitia, Doctor.

Chasuble. [Bowing.] A classical allusion merely, drawn from the Pagan authors. I shall see you both no doubt at Evensong?

Miss Prism. I think, dear Doctor, I will have a stroll with you. I find I have a headache after all, and a walk might do it good.

Chasuble. With pleasure, Miss Prism, with pleasure. We might go as far as the schools and back.

Miss Prism. That would be delightful. Cecily, you will read your Political Economy in my absence. The chapter on the Fall of the Rupee you may omit. It is somewhat too sensational. Even these metallic problems have their melodramatic side.

[Goes down the garden with Dr. Chasuble.]

Cecily. [Picks up books and throws them back on table.] Horrid Political Economy! Horrid Geography! Horrid, horrid German!

[Enter Merriman with a card on a salver.]

Merriman. Mr. Ernest Worthing has just driven over from the station. He has brought his luggage with him.

Cecily. [Takes the card and reads it.] 'Mr. Ernest Worthing, B. 4, The Albany, W.' Uncle Jack's brother! Did you tell him Mr. Worthing was in town?

Merriman. Yes, Miss. He seemed very much disappointed. I mentioned that you and Miss Prism were in the garden. He said he was anxious to speak to you privately for a moment.

Cecily. Ask Mr. Ernest Worthing to come here. I suppose you had better talk to the housekeeper about a room for him.

Merriman. Yes, Miss.

[Merriman goes off.]

Cecily. I have never met any really wicked person before. I feel rather frightened. I am so afraid he will look just like every one else.

[Enter Algernon, very gay and debonnair.] He does!

Algernon. [Raising his hat.] You are my little cousin Cecily, I'm sure.

Cecily. You are under some strange mistake. I am not little. In fact, I believe I am more than usually tall for my age. [Algernon is rather taken aback.] But I am your cousin Cecily. You, I see from your card, are Uncle Jack's brother, my cousin Ernest, my wicked cousin Ernest.

Algernon. Oh! I am not really wicked at all, cousin Cecily. You mustn't think that I am wicked.

Cecily. If you are not, then you have certainly been deceiving us all in a very inexcusable manner. I hope you have not been leading a double life, pretending to be wicked and being really good all the time. That would be hypocrisy.

Algernon. [Looks at her in amazement.] Oh! Of course I have been rather reckless.

Cecily. I am glad to hear it.

Algernon. In fact, now you mention the subject, I have been very bad in my own small way.

Cecily. I don't think you should be so proud of that, though I am sure it must have been very pleasant.

Algernon. It is much pleasanter being here with you.

Cecily. I can't understand how you are here at all. Uncle Jack won't be back till Monday afternoon.

Algernon. That is a great disappointment. I am obliged to go up by the first train on Monday morning. I have a business appointment that I am anxious . . . to miss?

Cecily. Couldn't you miss it anywhere but in London?

Algernon. No: the appointment is in London.

Cecily. Well, I know, of course, how important it is not to keep a business engagement, if one wants to retain any sense of the beauty of life, but still I think you had better wait till Uncle Jack arrives. I know he wants to speak to you about your emigrating.

Algernon. About my what?

Cecily. Your emigrating. He has gone up to buy your outfit.

Algernon. I certainly wouldn't let Jack buy my outfit. He has no taste in neckties at all.

Cecily. I don't think you will require neckties. Uncle Jack is sending you to Australia.

Algernon. Australia! I'd sooner die.

Cecily. Well, he said at dinner on Wednesday night, that you would have to choose between this world, the next world, and Australia.

Algernon. Oh, well! The accounts I have received of Australia and the next world, are not particularly encouraging. This world is good enough for me, cousin Cecily.

Cecily. Yes, but are you good enough for it?

Algernon. I'm afraid I'm not that. That is why I want you to reform me. You might make that your mission, if you don't mind, cousin Cecily.

Cecily. I'm afraid I've no time, this afternoon.

Algernon. Well, would you mind my reforming myself this afternoon?

Cecily. It is rather Quixotic of you. But I think you should try.

Algernon. I will. I feel better already.

Cecily. You are looking a little worse.

Algernon. That is because I am hungry.

Cecily. How thoughtless of me. I should have remembered that when one is going to lead an entirely new life, one requires regular and wholesome meals. Won't you come in?

Algernon. Thank you. Might I have a buttonhole first? I never have any appetite unless I have a buttonhole first.

Cecily. A Marechal Niel? [Picks up scissors.]

Algernon. No, I'd sooner have a pink rose.

Cecily. Why? [Cuts a flower.]

Algernon. Because you are like a pink rose, Cousin Cecily.

Cecily. I don't think it can be right for you to talk to me like that. Miss Prism never says such things to me.

Algernon. Then Miss Prism is a short-sighted old lady. [Cecily puts the rose in his buttonhole.] You are the prettiest girl I ever saw.

Cecily. Miss Prism says that all good looks are a snare.

Algernon. They are a snare that every sensible man would like to be caught in.

Cecily. Oh, I don't think I would care to catch a sensible man. I shouldn't know what to talk to him about.

[They pass into the house. Miss Prism and Dr. Chasuble return.]

Miss Prism. You are too much alone, dear Dr. Chasuble. You should get married. A misanthrope I can understand--a womanthrope, never!

Chasuble. [With a scholar's shudder.] Believe me, I do not deserve so neologistic a phrase. The precept as well as the practice of the Primitive Church was distinctly against matrimony.

Miss Prism. [Sententiously.] That is obviously the reason why the Primitive Church has not lasted up to the present day. And you do not seem to realise, dear Doctor, that by persistently remaining single, a man converts himself into a permanent public temptation. Men should be more careful; this very celibacy leads weaker vessels astray.

Chasuble. But is a man not equally attractive when married?

Miss Prism. No married man is ever attractive except to his wife.

Chasuble. And often, I've been told, not even to her.

Miss Prism. That depends on the intellectual sympathies of the woman. Maturity can always be depended on. Ripeness can be trusted. Young women are green. [Dr. Chasuble starts.] I spoke horticulturally. My metaphor was drawn from fruits. But where is Cecily?

Chasuble. Perhaps she followed us to the schools.

[Enter Jack slowly from the back of the garden. He is dressed in the deepest mourning, with crape hatband and black gloves.]

Miss Prism. Mr. Worthing!

Chasuble. Mr. Worthing?

Miss Prism. This is indeed a surprise. We did not look for you till Monday afternoon.

Jack. [Shakes Miss Prism's hand in a tragic manner.] I have returned sooner than I expected. Dr. Chasuble, I hope you are well?

Chasuble. Dear Mr. Worthing, I trust this garb of woe does not betoken some terrible calamity?

Jack. My brother.

Miss Prism. More shameful debts and extravagance?

Chasuble. Still leading his life of pleasure?

Jack. [Shaking his head.] Dead!

Chasuble. Your brother Ernest dead?

Jack. Quite dead.

Miss Prism. What a lesson for him! I trust he will profit by it.

Chasuble. Mr. Worthing, I offer you my sincere condolence. You have at least the consolation of knowing that you were always the most generous and forgiving of brothers.

Jack. Poor Ernest! He had many faults, but it is a sad, sad blow.

Chasuble. Very sad indeed. Were you with him at the end?

Jack. No. He died abroad; in Paris, in fact. I had a telegram last night from the manager of the Grand Hotel.

Chasuble. Was the cause of death mentioned?

Jack. A severe chill, it seems.

Miss Prism. As a man sows, so shall he reap.

Chasuble. [Raising his hand.] Charity, dear Miss Prism, charity! None of us are perfect. I myself am peculiarly susceptible to draughts. Will the interment take place here?

Jack. No. He seems to have expressed a desire to be buried in Paris.

Chasuble. In Paris! [Shakes his head.] I fear that hardly points to any very serious state of mind at the last. You would no doubt wish me to make some slight allusion to this tragic domestic affliction next Sunday. [Jack presses his hand convulsively.] My sermon on the meaning of the manna in the wilderness can be adapted to almost any occasion, joyful, or, as in the present case, distressing. [All sigh.] I have preached it at harvest celebrations, christenings, confirmations, on days of humiliation and festal days. The last time I delivered it was in the Cathedral, as a charity sermon on behalf of the Society for the Prevention of Discontent among the Upper Orders. The Bishop, who was present, was much struck by some of the analogies I drew.

Jack. Ah! that reminds me, you mentioned christenings I think, Dr. Chasuble? I suppose you know how to christen all right? [Dr. Chasuble looks astounded.] I mean, of course, you are continually christening, aren't you?

Miss Prism. It is, I regret to say, one of the Rector's most constant duties in this parish. I have often spoken to the poorer classes on the subject. But they don't seem to know what thrift is.

Chasuble. But is there any particular infant in whom you are interested, Mr. Worthing? Your brother was, I believe, unmarried, was he not?

Jack. Oh yes.

Miss Prism. [Bitterly.] People who live entirely for pleasure usually are.

Jack. But it is not for any child, dear Doctor. I am very fond of children. No! the fact is, I would like to be christened myself, this afternoon, if you have nothing better to do.

Chasuble. But surely, Mr. Worthing, you have been christened already?

Jack. I don't remember anything about it.

Chasuble. But have you any grave doubts on the subject?

Jack. I certainly intend to have. Of course I don't know if the thing would bother you in any way, or if you think I am a little too old now.

Chasuble. Not at all. The sprinkling, and, indeed, the immersion of adults is a perfectly canonical practice.

Jack. Immersion!

Chasuble. You need have no apprehensions. Sprinkling is all that is necessary, or indeed I think advisable. Our weather is so changeable. At what hour would you wish the ceremony performed?

Jack. Oh, I might trot round about five if that would suit you.

Chasuble. Perfectly, perfectly! In fact I have two similar ceremonies to perform at that time. A case of twins that occurred recently in one of the outlying cottages on your own estate. Poor Jenkins the carter, a most hard-working man.

Jack. Oh! I don't see much fun in being christened along with other babies. It would be childish. Would half-past five do?

Chasuble. Admirably! Admirably! [Takes out watch.] And now, dear Mr. Worthing, I will not intrude any longer into a house of sorrow. I would merely beg you not to be too much bowed down by grief. What seem to us bitter trials are often blessings in disguise.

Miss Prism. This seems to me a blessing of an extremely obvious kind.

[Enter Cecily from the house.]

Cecily. Uncle Jack! Oh, I am pleased to see you back. But what horrid clothes you have got on! Do go and change them.

Miss Prism. Cecily!

Chasuble. My child! my child! [Cecily goes towards Jack; he kisses her brow in a melancholy manner.]

Cecily. What is the matter, Uncle Jack? Do look happy! You look as if you had toothache, and I have got such a surprise for you. Who do you think is in the dining-room? Your brother!

Jack. Who?

Cecily. Your brother Ernest. He arrived about half an hour ago.

Jack. What nonsense! I haven't got a brother.

Cecily. Oh, don't say that. However badly he may have behaved to you in the past he is still your brother. You couldn't be so heartless as to disown him. I'll tell him to come out. And you will shake hands with him, won't you, Uncle Jack? [Runs back into the house.]

Chasuble. These are very joyful tidings.

Miss Prism. After we had all been resigned to his loss, his sudden return seems to me peculiarly distressing.

Jack. My brother is in the dining-room? I don't know what it all means. I think it is perfectly absurd.

[Enter Algernon and Cecily hand in hand. They come slowly up to Jack.]

Jack. Good heavens! [Motions Algernon away.]

Algernon. Brother John, I have come down from town to tell you that I am very sorry for all the trouble I have given you, and that I intend to lead a better life in the future. [Jack glares at him and does not take his hand.]

Cecily. Uncle Jack, you are not going to refuse your own brother's hand?

Jack. Nothing will induce me to take his hand. I think his coming down here disgraceful. He knows perfectly well why.

Cecily. Uncle Jack, do be nice. There is some good in every one. Ernest has just been telling me about his poor invalid friend Mr. Bunbury whom he goes to visit so often. And surely there must be much good in one who is kind to an invalid, and leaves the pleasures of London to sit by a bed of pain.

Jack. Oh! he has been talking about Bunbury, has he?

Cecily. Yes, he has told me all about poor Mr. Bunbury, and his terrible state of health.

Jack. Bunbury! Well, I won't have him talk to you about Bunbury or about anything else. It is enough to drive one perfectly frantic.

Algernon. Of course I admit that the faults were all on my side. But I must say that I think that Brother John's coldness to me is peculiarly painful. I expected a more enthusiastic welcome, especially considering it is the first time I have come here.

Cecily. Uncle Jack, if you don't shake hands with Ernest I will never forgive you.

Jack. Never forgive me?

Cecily. Never, never, never!

Jack. Well, this is the last time I shall ever do it. [Shakes with Algernon and glares.]

Chasuble. It's pleasant, is it not, to see so perfect a reconciliation? I think we might leave the two brothers together.

Miss Prism. Cecily, you will come with us.

Cecily. Certainly, Miss Prism. My little task of reconciliation is over.

Chasuble. You have done a beautiful action to-day, dear child.

Miss Prism. We must not be premature in our judgments.

Cecily. I feel very happy. [They all go off except Jack and Algernon.]

Jack. You young scoundrel, Algy, you must get out of this place as soon as possible. I don't allow any Bunburying here.

[Enter Merriman.]

Merriman. I have put Mr. Ernest's things in the room next to yours, sir. I suppose that is all right?

Jack. What?

Merriman. Mr. Ernest's luggage, sir. I have unpacked it and put it in the room next to your own.

Jack. His luggage?

Merriman. Yes, sir. Three portmanteaus, a dressing-case, two hat-boxes, and a large luncheon-basket.

Algernon. I am afraid I can't stay more than a week this time.

Jack. Merriman, order the dog-cart at once. Mr. Ernest has been suddenly called back to town.

Merriman. Yes, sir. [Goes back into the house.]

Algernon. What a fearful liar you are, Jack. I have not been called back to town at all.

Jack. Yes, you have.

Algernon. I haven't heard any one call me.

Jack. Your duty as a gentleman calls you back.

Algernon. My duty as a gentleman has never interfered with my pleasures in the smallest degree.

Jack. I can quite understand that.

Algernon. Well, Cecily is a darling.

Jack. You are not to talk of Miss Cardew like that. I don't like it.

Algernon. Well, I don't like your clothes. You look perfectly ridiculous in them. Why on earth don't you go up and change? It is perfectly childish to be in deep mourning for a man who is actually staying for a whole week with you in your house as a guest. I call it grotesque.

Jack. You are certainly not staying with me for a whole week as a guest or anything else. You have got to leave . . . by the four-five train.

Algernon. I certainly won't leave you so long as you are in mourning. It would be most unfriendly. If I were in mourning you would stay with me, I suppose. I should think it very unkind if you didn't.

Jack. Well, will you go if I change my clothes?

Algernon. Yes, if you are not too long. I never saw anybody take so long to dress, and with such little result.

Jack. Well, at any rate, that is better than being always over-dressed as you are.

Algernon. If I am occasionally a little over-dressed, I make up for it by being always immensely over-educated.

Jack. Your vanity is ridiculous, your conduct an outrage, and your presence in my garden utterly absurd. However, you have got to catch the four-five, and I hope you will have a pleasant journey back to town. This Bunburying, as you call it, has not been a great success for you.

[Goes into the house.]

Algernon. I think it has been a great success. I'm in love with Cecily, and that is everything.

[Enter Cecily at the back of the garden. She picks up the can and begins to water the flowers.] But I must see her before I go, and make arrangements for another Bunbury. Ah, there she is.

Cecily. Oh, I merely came back to water the roses. I thought you were with Uncle Jack.

Algernon. He's gone to order the dog-cart for me.

Cecily. Oh, is he going to take you for a nice drive?

Algernon. He's going to send me away.

Cecily. Then have we got to part?

Algernon. I am afraid so. It's a very painful parting.

Cecily. It is always painful to part from people whom one has known for a very brief space of time. The absence of old friends one can endure with equanimity. But even a momentary separation from anyone to whom one has just been introduced is almost unbearable.

Algernon. Thank you.

[Enter Merriman.]

Merriman. The dog-cart is at the door, sir. [Algernon looks appealingly at Cecily.]

Cecily. It can wait, Merriman for . . . five minutes.

Merriman. Yes, Miss. [Exit Merriman.]

Algernon. I hope, Cecily, I shall not offend you if I state quite frankly and openly that you seem to me to be in every way the visible personification of absolute perfection.

Cecily. I think your frankness does you great credit, Ernest. If you will allow me, I will copy your remarks into my diary. [Goes over to table and begins writing in diary.]

Algernon. Do you really keep a diary? I'd give anything to look at it. May I?

Cecily. Oh no. [Puts her hand over it.] You see, it is simply a very young girl's record of her own thoughts and impressions, and consequently meant for publication. When it appears in volume form I hope you will order a copy. But pray, Ernest, don't stop. I delight in taking down from dictation. I have reached 'absolute perfection'. You can go on. I am quite ready for more.

Algernon. [Somewhat taken aback.] Ahem! Ahem!

Cecily. Oh, don't cough, Ernest. When one is dictating one should speak fluently and not cough. Besides, I don't know how to spell a cough. [Writes as Algernon speaks.]

Algernon. [Speaking very rapidly.] Cecily, ever since I first looked upon your wonderful and incomparable beauty, I have dared to love you wildly, passionately, devotedly, hopelessly.

Cecily. I don't think that you should tell me that you love me wildly, passionately, devotedly, hopelessly. Hopelessly doesn't seem to make much sense, does it?

Algernon. Cecily!

[Enter Merriman.]

Merriman. The dog-cart is waiting, sir.

Algernon. Tell it to come round next week, at the same hour.

Merriman. [Looks at Cecily, who makes no sign.] Yes, sir.

[Merriman retires.]

Cecily. Uncle Jack would be very much annoyed if he knew you were staying on till next week, at the same hour.

Algernon. Oh, I don't care about Jack. I don't care for anybody in the whole world but you. I love you, Cecily. You will marry me, won't you?

Cecily. You silly boy! Of course. Why, we have been engaged for the last three months.

Algernon. For the last three months?

Cecily. Yes, it will be exactly three months on Thursday.

Algernon. But how did we become engaged?

Cecily. Well, ever since dear Uncle Jack first confessed to us that he had a younger brother who was very wicked and bad, you of course have formed the chief topic of conversation between myself and Miss Prism. And of course a man who is much talked about is always very attractive. One feels there must be something in him, after all. I daresay it was foolish of me, but I fell in love with you, Ernest.

Algernon. Darling! And when was the engagement actually settled?

Cecily. On the 14th of February last. Worn out by your entire ignorance of my existence, I determined to end the matter one way or the other, and after a long struggle with myself I accepted you under this dear old tree here. The next day I bought this little ring in your name, and this is the little bangle with the true lover's knot I promised you always to wear.

Algernon. Did I give you this? It's very pretty, isn't it?

Cecily. Yes, you've wonderfully good taste, Ernest. It's the excuse I've always given for your leading such a bad life. And this is the box in which I keep all your dear letters. [Kneels at table, opens box, and produces letters tied up with blue ribbon.]

Algernon. My letters! But, my own sweet Cecily, I have never written you any letters.

Cecily. You need hardly remind me of that, Ernest. I remember only too well that I was forced to write your letters for you. I wrote always three times a week, and sometimes oftener.

Algernon. Oh, do let me read them, Cecily?

Cecily. Oh, I couldn't possibly. They would make you far too conceited. [Replaces box.] The three you wrote me after I had broken off the engagement are so beautiful, and so badly spelled, that even now I can hardly read them without crying a little.

Algernon. But was our engagement ever broken off?

Cecily. Of course it was. On the 22nd of last March. You can see the entry if you like. [Shows diary.] 'To-day I broke off my engagement with Ernest. I feel it is better to do so. The weather still continues charming.'

Algernon. But why on earth did you break it off? What had I done? I had done nothing at all. Cecily, I am very much hurt indeed to hear you broke it off. Particularly when the weather was so charming.

Cecily. It would hardly have been a really serious engagement if it hadn't been broken off at least once. But I forgave you before the week was out.

Algernon. [Crossing to her, and kneeling.] What a perfect angel you are, Cecily.

Cecily. You dear romantic boy. [He kisses her, she puts her fingers through his hair.] I hope your hair curls naturally, does it?

Algernon. Yes, darling, with a little help from others.

Cecily. I am so glad.

Algernon. You'll never break off our engagement again, Cecily?

Cecily. I don't think I could break it off now that I have actually met you. Besides, of course, there is the question of your name.

Algernon. Yes, of course. [Nervously.]

Cecily. You must not laugh at me, darling, but it had always been a girlish dream of mine to love some one whose name was Ernest. [Algernon rises, Cecily also.] There is something in that name that seems to inspire absolute confidence. I pity any poor married woman whose husband is not called Ernest.

Algernon. But, my dear child, do you mean to say you could not love me if I had some other name?

Cecily. But what name?

Algernon. Oh, any name you like--Algernon--for instance . . .

Cecily. But I don't like the name of Algernon.

Algernon. Well, my own dear, sweet, loving little darling, I really can't see why you should object to the name of Algernon. It is not at all a bad name. In fact, it is rather an aristocratic name. Half of the chaps who get into the Bankruptcy Court are called Algernon. But seriously, Cecily . . . [Moving to her] . . . if my name was Algy, couldn't you love me?

Cecily. [Rising.] I might respect you, Ernest, I might admire your character, but I fear that I should not be able to give you my undivided attention.

Algernon. Ahem! Cecily! [Picking up hat.] Your Rector here is, I suppose, thoroughly experienced in the practice of all the rites and ceremonials of the Church?

Cecily. Oh, yes. Dr. Chasuble is a most learned man. He has never written a single book, so you can imagine how much he knows.

Algernon. I must see him at once on a most important christening--I mean on most important business.

Cecily. Oh!

Algernon. I shan't be away more than half an hour.

Cecily. Considering that we have been engaged since February the 14th, and that I only met you to-day for the first time, I think it is rather hard that you should leave me for so long a period as half an hour. Couldn't you make it twenty minutes?

Algernon. I'll be back in no time.

[Kisses her and rushes down the garden.]

Cecily. What an impetuous boy he is! I like his hair so much. I must enter his proposal in my diary.

[Enter Merriman.]

Merriman. A Miss Fairfax has just called to see Mr. Worthing. On very important business, Miss Fairfax states.

Cecily. Isn't Mr. Worthing in his library?

Merriman. Mr. Worthing went over in the direction of the Rectory some time ago.

Cecily. Pray ask the lady to come out here; Mr. Worthing is sure to be back soon. And you can bring tea.

Merriman. Yes, Miss. [Goes out.]

Cecily. Miss Fairfax! I suppose one of the many good elderly women who are associated with Uncle Jack in some of his philanthropic work in London. I don't quite like women who are interested in philanthropic work. I think it is so forward of them.

[Enter Merriman.]

Merriman. Miss Fairfax.

[Enter Gwendolen.]

[Exit Merriman.]

Cecily. [Advancing to meet her.] Pray let me introduce myself to you. My name is Cecily Cardew.

Gwendolen. Cecily Cardew? [Moving to her and shaking hands.] What a very sweet name! Something tells me that we are going to be great friends. I like you already more than I can say. My first impressions of people are never wrong.

Cecily. How nice of you to like me so much after we have known each other such a comparatively short time. Pray sit down.

Gwendolen. [Still standing up.] I may call you Cecily, may I not?

Cecily. With pleasure!

Gwendolen. And you will always call me Gwendolen, won't you?

Cecily. If you wish.

Gwendolen. Then that is all quite settled, is it not?

Cecily. I hope so. [A pause. They both sit down together.]

Gwendolen. Perhaps this might be a favourable opportunity for my mentioning who I am. My father is Lord Bracknell. You have never heard of papa, I suppose?

Cecily. I don't think so.

Gwendolen. Outside the family circle, papa, I am glad to say, is entirely unknown. I think that is quite as it should be. The home seems to me to be the proper sphere for the man. And certainly once a man begins to neglect his domestic duties he becomes painfully effeminate, does he not? And I don't like that. It makes men so very attractive. Cecily, mamma, whose views on education are remarkably strict, has brought me up to be extremely short-sighted; it is part of her system; so do you mind my looking at you through my glasses?

Cecily. Oh! not at all, Gwendolen. I am very fond of being looked at.

Gwendolen. [After examining Cecily carefully through a lorgnette.] You are here on a short visit, I suppose.

Cecily. Oh no! I live here.

Gwendolen. [Severely.] Really? Your mother, no doubt, or some female relative of advanced years, resides here also?

Cecily. Oh no! I have no mother, nor, in fact, any relations.

Gwendolen. Indeed?

Cecily. My dear guardian, with the assistance of Miss Prism, has the arduous task of looking after me.

Gwendolen. Your guardian?

Cecily. Yes, I am Mr. Worthing's ward.

Gwendolen. Oh! It is strange he never mentioned to me that he had a ward. How secretive of him! He grows more interesting hourly. I am not sure, however, that the news inspires me with feelings of unmixed delight. [Rising and going to her.] I am very fond of you, Cecily; I have liked you ever since I met you! But I am bound to state that now that I know that you are Mr. Worthing's ward, I cannot help expressing a wish you were--well, just a little older than you seem to be--and not quite so very alluring in appearance. In fact, if I may speak candidly--

Cecily. Pray do! I think that whenever one has anything unpleasant to say, one should always be quite candid.

Gwendolen. Well, to speak with perfect candour, Cecily, I wish that you were fully forty-two, and more than usually plain for your age. Ernest has a strong upright nature. He is the very soul of truth and honour. Disloyalty would be as impossible to him as deception. But even men of the noblest possible moral character are extremely susceptible to the influence of the physical charms of others. Modern, no less than Ancient History, supplies us with many most painful examples of what I refer to. If it were not so, indeed, History would be quite unreadable.

Cecily. I beg your pardon, Gwendolen, did you say Ernest?

Gwendolen. Yes.

Cecily. Oh, but it is not Mr. Ernest Worthing who is my guardian. It is his brother--his elder brother.

Gwendolen. [Sitting down again.] Ernest never mentioned to me that he had a brother.

Cecily. I am sorry to say they have not been on good terms for a long time.

Gwendolen. Ah! that accounts for it. And now that I think of it I have never heard any man mention his brother. The subject seems distasteful to most men. Cecily, you have lifted a load from my mind. I was growing almost anxious. It would have been terrible if any cloud had come across a friendship like ours, would it not? Of course you are quite, quite sure that it is not Mr. Ernest Worthing who is your guardian?

Cecily. Quite sure. [A pause.] In fact, I am going to be his.

Gwendolen. [Inquiringly.] I beg your pardon?

Cecily. [Rather shy and confidingly.] Dearest Gwendolen, there is no reason why I should make a secret of it to you. Our little county newspaper is sure to chronicle the fact next week. Mr. Ernest Worthing and I are engaged to be married.

Gwendolen. [Quite politely, rising.] My darling Cecily, I think there must be some slight error. Mr. Ernest Worthing is engaged to me. The announcement will appear in the *Morning Post* on Saturday at the latest.

Cecily. [Very politely, rising.] I am afraid you must be under some misconception. Ernest proposed to me exactly ten minutes ago. [Shows diary.]

Gwendolen. [Examines diary through her lorgnettte carefully.] It is certainly very curious, for he asked me to be his wife yesterday afternoon at 5.30. If you would care to verify the incident, pray do so. [Produces diary of her own.] I never travel without my diary. One should always have something sensational to read in the train. I am so sorry, dear Cecily, if it is any disappointment to you, but I am afraid I have the prior claim.

Cecily. It would distress me more than I can tell you, dear Gwendolen, if it caused you any mental or physical anguish, but I feel bound to point out that since Ernest proposed to you he clearly has changed his mind.

Gwendolen. [Meditatively.] If the poor fellow has been entrapped into any foolish promise I shall consider it my duty to rescue him at once, and with a firm hand.

Cecily. [Thoughtfully and sadly.] Whatever unfortunate entanglement my dear boy may have got into, I will never reproach him with it after we are married.

Gwendolen. Do you allude to me, Miss Cardew, as an entanglement? You are presumptuous. On an occasion of this kind it becomes more than a moral duty to speak one's mind. It becomes a pleasure.

Cecily. Do you suggest, Miss Fairfax, that I entrapped Ernest into an engagement? How dare you? This is no time for wearing the shallow mask of manners. When I see a spade I call it a spade.

Gwendolen. [Satirically.] I am glad to say that I have never seen a spade. It is obvious that our social spheres have been widely different.

[Enter Merriman, followed by the footman. He carries a salver, table cloth, and plate stand. Cecily is about to retort. The presence of the servants exercises a restraining influence, under which both girls chafe.]

Merriman. Shall I lay tea here as usual, Miss?

Cecily. [Sternly, in a calm voice.] Yes, as usual. [Merriman begins to clear table and lay cloth. A long pause. Cecily and Gwendolen glare at each other.]

Gwendolen. Are there many interesting walks in the vicinity, Miss Cardew?

Cecily. Oh! yes! a great many. From the top of one of the hills quite close one can see five counties.

Gwendolen. Five counties! I don't think I should like that; I hate crowds.

Cecily. [Sweetly.] I suppose that is why you live in town? [Gwendolen bites her lip, and beats her foot nervously with her parasol.]

Gwendolen. [Looking round.] Quite a well-kept garden this is, Miss Cardew.

Cecily. So glad you like it, Miss Fairfax.

Gwendolen. I had no idea there were any flowers in the country.

Cecily. Oh, flowers are as common here, Miss Fairfax, as people are in London.

Gwendolen. Personally I cannot understand how anybody manages to exist in the country, if anybody who is anybody does. The country always bores me to death.

Cecily. Ah! This is what the newspapers call agricultural depression, is it not? I believe the aristocracy are suffering very much from it just at present. It is almost an epidemic amongst them, I have been told. May I offer you some tea, Miss Fairfax?

Gwendolen. [With elaborate politeness.] Thank you. [Aside.] Detestable girl! But I require tea!

Cecily. [Sweetly.] Sugar?

Gwendolen. [Superciliously.] No, thank you. Sugar is not fashionable any more. [Cecily looks angrily at her, takes up the tongs and puts four lumps of sugar into the cup.]

Cecily. [Severely.] Cake or bread and butter?

Gwendolen. [In a bored manner.] Bread and butter, please. Cake is rarely seen at the best houses nowadays.

Cecily. [Cuts a very large slice of cake, and puts it on the tray.] Hand that to Miss Fairfax.

[Merriman does so, and goes out with footman. Gwendolen drinks the tea and makes a grimace. Puts down cup at once, reaches out her hand to the bread and butter, looks at it, and finds it is cake. Rises in indignation.]

Gwendolen. You have filled my tea with lumps of sugar, and though I asked most distinctly for bread and butter, you have given me cake. I am known for the gentleness of my disposition, and the extraordinary sweetness of my nature, but I warn you, Miss Cardew, you may go too far.

Cecily. [Rising.] To save my poor, innocent, trusting boy from the machinations of any other girl there are no lengths to which I would not go.

Gwendolen. From the moment I saw you I distrusted you. I felt that you were false and deceitful. I am never deceived in such matters. My first impressions of people are invariably right.

Cecily. It seems to me, Miss Fairfax, that I am trespassing on your valuable time. No doubt you have many other calls of a similar character to make in the neighbourhood.

[Enter Jack.]

Gwendolen. [Catching sight of him.] Ernest! My own Ernest!

Jack. Gwendolen! Darling! [Offers to kiss her.]

Gwendolen. [Draws back.] A moment! May I ask if you are engaged to be married to this young lady? [Points to Cecily.]

Jack. [Laughing.] To dear little Cecily! Of course not! What could have put such an idea into your pretty little head?

Gwendolen. Thank you. You may! [Offers her cheek.]

Cecily. [Very sweetly.] I knew there must be some misunderstanding, Miss Fairfax. The gentleman whose arm is at present round your waist is my guardian, Mr. John Worthing.

Gwendolen. I beg your pardon?

Cecily. This is Uncle Jack.

Gwendolen. [Receding.] Jack! Oh!

[Enter Algernon.]

Cecily. Here is Ernest.

Algernon. [Goes straight over to Cecily without noticing any one else.] My own love! [Offers to kiss her.]

Cecily. [Drawing back.] A moment, Ernest! May I ask you--are you engaged to be married to this young lady?

Algernon. [Looking round.] To what young lady? Good heavens! Gwendolen!

Cecily. Yes! to good heavens, Gwendolen, I mean to Gwendolen.

Algernon. [Laughing.] Of course not! What could have put such an idea into your pretty little head?

Cecily. Thank you. [Presenting her cheek to be kissed.] You may. [Algernon kisses her.]

Gwendolen. I felt there was some slight error, Miss Cardew. The gentleman who is now embracing you is my cousin, Mr. Algernon Moncrieff.

Cecily. [Breaking away from Algernon.] Algernon Moncrieff! Oh! [The two girls move towards each other and put their arms round each other's waists as if for protection.]

Cecily. Are you called Algernon?

Algernon. I cannot deny it.

Cecily. Oh!

Gwendolen. Is your name really John?

Jack. [Standing rather proudly.] I could deny it if I liked. I could deny anything if I liked. But my name certainly is John. It has been John for years.

Cecily. [To Gwendolen.] A gross deception has been practised on both of us.

Gwendolen. My poor wounded Cecily!

Cecily. My sweet wronged Gwendolen!

Gwendolen. [Slowly and seriously.] You will call me sister, will you not? [They embrace. Jack and Algernon groan and walk up and down.]

Cecily. [Rather brightly.] There is just one question I would like to be allowed to ask my guardian.

Gwendolen. An admirable idea! Mr. Worthing, there is just one question I would like to be permitted to put to you. Where is your brother Ernest? We are both engaged to be married to your brother Ernest, so it is a matter of some importance to us to know where your brother Ernest is at present.

Jack. [Slowly and hesitatingly.] Gwendolen--Cecily--it is very painful for me to be forced to speak the truth. It is the first time in my life that I have ever been reduced to such a painful position, and I am really quite inexperienced in doing anything of the kind. However, I will tell you quite frankly that I have no brother Ernest. I have no brother at all. I never had a brother in my life, and I certainly have not the smallest intention of ever having one in the future.

Cecily. [Surprised.] No brother at all?

Jack. [Cheerily.] None!

Gwendolen. [Severely.] Had you never a brother of any kind?

Jack. [Pleasantly.] Never. Not even of an kind.

Gwendolen. I am afraid it is quite clear, Cecily, that neither of us is engaged to be married to any one.

Cecily. It is not a very pleasant position for a young girl suddenly to find herself in. Is it?

Gwendolen. Let us go into the house. They will hardly venture to come after us there.

Cecily. No, men are so cowardly, aren't they?

[They retire into the house with scornful looks.]

Jack. This ghastly state of things is what you call Bunburying, I suppose?

Algernon. Yes, and a perfectly wonderful Bunbury it is. The most wonderful Bunbury I have ever had in my life.

Jack. Well, you've no right whatsoever to Bunbury here.

Algernon. That is absurd. One has a right to Bunbury anywhere one chooses. Every serious Bunburyist knows that.

Jack. Serious Bunburyist! Good heavens!

Algernon. Well, one must be serious about something, if one wants to have any amusement in life. I happen to be serious about Bunburying. What on earth you are serious about I haven't got the remotest idea. About everything, I should fancy. You have such an absolutely trivial nature.

Jack. Well, the only small satisfaction I have in the whole of this wretched business is that your friend Bunbury is quite exploded. You won't be able to run down to the country quite so often as you used to do, dear Algy. And a very good thing too.

Algernon. Your brother is a little off colour, isn't he, dear Jack? You won't be able to disappear to London quite so frequently as your wicked custom was. And not a bad thing either.

Jack. As for your conduct towards Miss Cardew, I must say that your taking in a sweet, simple, innocent girl like that is quite inexcusable. To say nothing of the fact that she is my ward.

Algernon. I can see no possible defence at all for your deceiving a brilliant, clever, thoroughly experienced young lady like Miss Fairfax. To say nothing of the fact that she is my cousin.

Jack. I wanted to be engaged to Gwendolen, that is all. I love her.

Algernon. Well, I simply wanted to be engaged to Cecily. I adore her.

Jack. There is certainly no chance of your marrying Miss Cardew.

Algernon. I don't think there is much likelihood, Jack, of you and Miss Fairfax being united.

Jack. Well, that is no business of yours.

Algernon. If it was my business, I wouldn't talk about it. [Begins to eat muffins.] It is very vulgar to talk about one's business. Only people like stock-brokers do that, and then merely at dinner parties.

Jack. How can you sit there, calmly eating muffins when we are in this horrible trouble, I can't make out. You seem to me to be perfectly heartless.

Algernon. Well, I can't eat muffins in an agitated manner. The butter would probably get on my cuffs. One should always eat muffins quite calmly. It is the only way to eat them.

Jack. I say it's perfectly heartless your eating muffins at all, under the circumstances.

106

Algernon. When I am in trouble, eating is the only thing that consoles me. Indeed, when I am in really great trouble, as any one who knows me intimately will tell you, I refuse everything except food and drink. At the present moment I am eating muffins because I am unhappy. Besides, I am particularly fond of muffins. [Rising.]

Jack. [Rising.] Well, that is no reason why you should eat them all in that greedy way. [Takes muffins from Algernon.]

Algernon. [Offering tea-cake.] I wish you would have tea-cake instead. I don't like tea-cake.

Jack. Good heavens! I suppose a man may eat his own muffins in his own garden.

Algernon. But you have just said it was perfectly heartless to eat muffins.

Jack. I said it was perfectly heartless of you, under the circumstances. That is a very different thing.

Algernon. That may be. But the muffins are the same. [He seizes the muffin-dish from Jack.]

Jack. Algy, I wish to goodness you would go.

Algernon. You can't possibly ask me to go without having some dinner. It's absurd. I never go without my dinner. No one ever does, except vegetarians and people like that. Besides I have just made arrangements with Dr. Chasuble to be christened at a quarter to six under the name of Ernest.

Jack. My dear fellow, the sooner you give up that nonsense the better. I made arrangements this morning with Dr. Chasuble to be christened myself at 5.30, and I naturally will take the name of Ernest. Gwendolen would wish it. We can't both be christened Ernest. It's absurd. Besides, I have a perfect right to be christened if I like. There is no evidence at all that I have ever been christened by anybody. I should think it extremely probable I never was, and so does Dr. Chasuble. It is entirely different in your case. You have been christened already.

Algernon. Yes, but I have not been christened for years.

Jack. Yes, but you have been christened. That is the important thing.

Algernon. Quite so. So I know my constitution can stand it. If you are not quite sure about your ever having been christened, I must say I think it rather dangerous your venturing on it now. It might make you very unwell. You can hardly have forgotten that some one very closely connected with you was very nearly carried off this week in Paris by a severe chill.

Jack. Yes, but you said yourself that a severe chill was not hereditary.

Algernon. It usen't to be, I know--but I daresay it is now. Science is always making wonderful improvements in things.

Jack. [Picking up the muffin-dish.] Oh, that is nonsense; you are always talking nonsense.

Algernon. Jack, you are at the muffins again! I wish you wouldn't. There are only two left. [Takes them.] I told you I was particularly fond of muffins.

Jack. But I hate tea-cake.

Algernon. Why on earth then do you allow tea-cake to be served up for your guests? What ideas you have of hospitality!

Jack. Algernon! I have already told you to go. I don't want you here. Why don't you go!

Algernon. I haven't quite finished my tea yet! and there is still one muffin left. [Jack groans, and sinks into a chair. Algernon still continues eating.]

ACT DROP

Third Act

SCENE

Morning-room at the Manor House.

[Gwendolen and Cecily are at the window, looking out into the garden.]

Gwendolen. The fact that they did not follow us at once into the house, as any one else would have done, seems to me to show that they have some sense of shame left.

Cecily. They have been eating muffins. That looks like repentance.

Gwendolen. [After a pause.] They don't seem to notice us at all. Couldn't you cough?

Cecily. But I haven't got a cough.

Gwendolen. They're looking at us. What effrontery!

Cecily. They're approaching. That's very forward of them.

Gwendolen. Let us preserve a dignified silence.

Cecily. Certainly. It's the only thing to do now. [Enter Jack followed by Algernon. They whistle some dreadful popular air from a British Opera.]

Gwendolen. This dignified silence seems to produce an unpleasant effect.

Cecily. A most distasteful one.

Gwendolen. But we will not be the first to speak.

Cecily. Certainly not.

Gwendolen. Mr. Worthing, I have something very particular to ask you. Much depends on your reply.

Cecily. Gwendolen, your common sense is invaluable. Mr. Moncrieff, kindly answer me the following question. Why did you pretend to be my guardian's brother?

Algernon. In order that I might have an opportunity of meeting you.

Cecily. [To Gwendolen.] That certainly seems a satisfactory explanation, does it not?

Gwendolen. Yes, dear, if you can believe him.

Cecily. I don't. But that does not affect the wonderful beauty of his answer.

Gwendolen. True. In matters of grave importance, style, not sincerity is the vital thing. Mr. Worthing, what explanation can you offer to me for pretending to have a brother? Was it in order that you might have an opportunity of coming up to town to see me as often as possible?

Jack. Can you doubt it, Miss Fairfax?

Gwendolen. I have the gravest doubts upon the subject. But I intend to crush them. This is not the moment for German scepticism. [Moving to Cecily.] Their explanations appear to be quite satisfactory, especially Mr. Worthing's. That seems to me to have the stamp of truth upon it.

Cecily. I am more than content with what Mr. Moncrieff said. His voice alone inspires one with absolute credulity.

Gwendolen. Then you think we should forgive them?

Cecily. Yes. I mean no.

Gwendolen. True! I had forgotten. There are principles at stake that one cannot surrender. Which of us should tell them? The task is not a pleasant one.

Cecily. Could we not both speak at the same time?

Gwendolen. An excellent idea! I nearly always speak at the same time as other people. Will you take the time from me?

Cecily. Certainly. [Gwendolen beats time with uplifted finger.]

Gwendolen and Cecily [Speaking together.] Your Christian names are still an insuperable barrier. That is all!

Jack and Algernon [Speaking together.] Our Christian names! Is that all? But we are going to be christened this afternoon.

Gwendolen. [To Jack.] For my sake you are prepared to do this terrible thing?

Jack. I am.

Cecily. [To Algernon.] To please me you are ready to face this fearful ordeal?

Algernon. I am!

Gwendolen. How absurd to talk of the equality of the sexes! Where questions of self-sacrifice are concerned, men are infinitely beyond us.

Jack. We are. [Clasps hands with Algernon.]

Cecily. They have moments of physical courage of which we women know absolutely nothing.

Gwendolen. [To Jack.] Darling!

Algernon. [To Cecily.] Darling! [They fall into each other's arms.]

[Enter Merriman. When he enters he coughs loudly, seeing the situation.]

Merriman. Ahem! Ahem! Lady Bracknell!

Jack. Good heavens!

[Enter Lady Bracknell. The couples separate in alarm. Exit Merriman.]

Lady Bracknell. Gwendolen! What does this mean?

Gwendolen. Merely that I am engaged to be married to Mr. Worthing, mamma.

Lady Bracknell. Come here. Sit down. Sit down immediately. Hesitation of any kind is a sign of mental decay in the young, of physical weakness in the old. [Turns to Jack.] Apprised, sir, of my daughter's sudden flight by her trusty maid, whose confidence I purchased by means of a small coin, I followed her at once by a luggage train. Her unhappy father is, I am glad to say, under the impression that she is attending a more than usually lengthy lecture by the University Extension Scheme on the Influence of a permanent income on Thought. I do not propose to undeceive him. Indeed I have never undeceived him on any question. I would consider it wrong. But of course, you will clearly understand that all communication between yourself and my daughter must cease immediately from this moment. On this point, as indeed on all points, I am firm.

Jack. I am engaged to be married to Gwendolen Lady Bracknell!

Lady Bracknell. You are nothing of the kind, sir. And now, as regards Algernon! . . . Algernon!

Algernon. Yes, Aunt Augusta.

Lady Bracknell. May I ask if it is in this house that your invalid friend Mr. Bunbury resides?

Algernon. [Stammering.] Oh! No! Bunbury doesn't live here. Bunbury is somewhere else at present. In fact, Bunbury is dead.

Lady Bracknell. Dead! When did Mr. Bunbury die? His death must have been extremely sudden.

Algernon. [Airily.] Oh! I killed Bunbury this afternoon. I mean poor Bunbury died this afternoon.

Lady Bracknell. What did he die of?

Algernon. Bunbury? Oh, he was quite exploded.

Lady Bracknell. Exploded! Was he the victim of a revolutionary outrage? I was not aware that Mr. Bunbury was interested in social legislation. If so, he is well punished for his morbidity.

Algernon. My dear Aunt Augusta, I mean he was found out! The doctors found out that Bunbury could not live, that is what I mean--so Bunbury died.

Lady Bracknell. He seems to have had great confidence in the opinion of his physicians. I am glad, however, that he made up his mind at the last to some definite course of action, and acted under proper medical advice. And now that we have finally got rid of this Mr. Bunbury, may I ask, Mr. Worthing, who is that young person whose hand my nephew Algernon is now holding in what seems to me a peculiarly unnecessary manner?

Jack. That lady is Miss Cecily Cardew, my ward. [Lady Bracknell bows coldly to Cecily.]

Algernon. I am engaged to be married to Cecily, Aunt Augusta.

Lady Bracknell. I beg your pardon?

Cecily. Mr. Moncrieff and I are engaged to be married, Lady Bracknell.

Lady Bracknell. [With a shiver, crossing to the sofa and sitting down.] I do not know whether there is anything peculiarly exciting in the air of this particular part of Hertfordshire, but the number of engagements that go on seems to me considerably above the proper average that statistics have laid down for our guidance. I think some preliminary inquiry on my part would not be out of place. Mr. Worthing, is Miss Cardew at all connected with any of the larger railway stations in London? I merely desire information. Until yesterday I had no idea that there were any families or persons whose origin was a Terminus. [Jack looks perfectly furious, but restrains himself.]

Jack. [In a clear, cold voice.] Miss Cardew is the grand-daughter of the late Mr. Thomas Cardew of 149 Belgrave Square, S.W.; Gervase Park, Dorking, Surrey; and the Sporran, Fifeshire, N.B.

Lady Bracknell. That sounds not unsatisfactory. Three addresses always inspire confidence, even in tradesmen. But what proof have I of their authenticity?

Jack. I have carefully preserved the Court Guides of the period. They are open to your inspection, Lady Bracknell.

Lady Bracknell. [Grimly.] I have known strange errors in that publication.

Jack. Miss Cardew's family solicitors are Messrs. Markby, Markby, and Markby.

Lady Bracknell. Markby, Markby, and Markby? A firm of the very highest position in their profession. Indeed I am told that one of the Mr. Markby's is occasionally to be seen at dinner parties. So far I am satisfied.

Jack. [Very irritably.] How extremely kind of you, Lady Bracknell! I have also in my possession, you will be pleased to hear, certificates of Miss Cardew's birth, baptism, whooping cough, registration, vaccination, confirmation, and the measles; both the German and the English variety.

Lady Bracknell. Ah! A life crowded with incident, I see; though perhaps somewhat too exciting for a young girl. I am not myself in favour of premature experiences. [Rises, looks at her watch.] Gwendolen! the time approaches for our departure. We have not a moment to lose. As a matter of form, Mr. Worthing, I had better ask you if Miss Cardew has any little fortune?

Jack. Oh! about a hundred and thirty thousand pounds in the Funds. That is all. Goodbye, Lady Bracknell. So pleased to have seen you.

Lady Bracknell. [Sitting down again.] A moment, Mr. Worthing. A hundred and thirty thousand pounds! And in the Funds! Miss Cardew seems to me a most attractive young lady, now that I look at her. Few girls of the present day have any really solid qualities, any of the qualities that last, and improve with time. We live, I regret to say, in an age of surfaces. [To Cecily.] Come over here, dear. [Cecily goes across.] Pretty child! your dress is sadly simple, and your hair seems almost as Nature might have left it. But we can soon alter all that. A thoroughly experienced French maid produces a really marvellous result in a very brief space of time. I remember recommending one to young Lady Lancing, and after three months her own husband did not know her.

Jack. And after six months nobody knew her.

Lady Bracknell. [Glares at Jack for a few moments. Then bends, with a practised smile, to Cecily.] Kindly turn round, sweet child. [Cecily turns completely round.] No, the side view is what I want. [Cecily presents her profile.] Yes, quite as I expected. There are distinct social possibilities in your profile. The two weak points in our age are its want of principle and its want of profile. The chin a little higher, dear. Style largely depends on the way the chin is worn. They are worn very high, just at present. Algernon!

Algernon. Yes, Aunt Augusta!

Lady Bracknell. There are distinct social possibilities in Miss Cardew's profile.

Algernon. Cecily is the sweetest, dearest, prettiest girl in the whole world. And I don't care twopence about social possibilities.

Lady Bracknell. Never speak disrespectfully of Society, Algernon. Only people who can't get into it do that. [To Cecily.] Dear child, of course you know that Algernon has nothing but his debts to depend upon. But I do not approve of mercenary marriages. When I married Lord Bracknell I had no fortune of any kind. But I never dreamed for a moment of allowing that to stand in my way. Well, I suppose I must give my consent.

Algernon. Thank you, Aunt Augusta.

Lady Bracknell. Cecily, you may kiss me!

Cecily. [Kisses her.] Thank you, Lady Bracknell.

Lady Bracknell. You may also address me as Aunt Augusta for the future.

Cecily. Thank you, Aunt Augusta.

Lady Bracknell. The marriage, I think, had better take place quite soon.

Algernon. Thank you, Aunt Augusta.

Cecily. Thank you, Aunt Augusta.

Lady Bracknell. To speak frankly, I am not in favour of long engagements. They give people the opportunity of finding out each other's character before marriage, which I think is never advisable.

Jack. I beg your pardon for interrupting you, Lady Bracknell, but this engagement is quite out of the question. I am Miss Cardew's guardian, and she cannot marry without my consent until she comes of age. That consent I absolutely decline to give.

Lady Bracknell. Upon what grounds may I ask? Algernon is an extremely, I may almost say an ostentatiously, eligible young man. He has nothing, but he looks everything. What more can one desire?

Jack. It pains me very much to have to speak frankly to you, Lady Bracknell, about your nephew, but the fact is that I do not approve at all of his moral character. I suspect him of being untruthful.
  [Algernon and Cecily look at him in indignant amazement.]

Lady Bracknell. Untruthful! My nephew Algernon? Impossible! He is an Oxonian.

Jack. I fear there can be no possible doubt about the matter. This afternoon during my temporary absence in London on an important question of romance, he obtained admission to my house by means of the false pretence of being my brother. Under an assumed name he drank, I've just been informed by my butler, an entire pint bottle of my Perrier-Jouet, Brut, '89; wine I was specially reserving for myself. Continuing his disgraceful deception, he succeeded in the course of the afternoon in alienating the affections of my only ward. He subsequently stayed to tea, and devoured every single muffin. And what makes his conduct all the more heartless is, that he was perfectly well aware from the first that I have no brother, that I never had a brother, and that I don't intend to have a brother, not even of any kind. I distinctly told him so myself yesterday afternoon.

Lady Bracknell. Ahem! Mr. Worthing, after careful consideration I have decided entirely to overlook my nephew's conduct to you.

Jack. That is very generous of you, Lady Bracknell. My own decision, however, is unalterable. I decline to give my consent.

Lady Bracknell. [To Cecily.] Come here, sweet child. [Cecily goes over.] How old are you, dear?

Cecily. Well, I am really only eighteen, but I always admit to twenty when I go to evening parties.

Lady Bracknell. You are perfectly right in making some slight alteration. Indeed, no woman should ever be quite accurate about her age. It looks so calculating . . . [In a meditative manner.] Eighteen, but admitting to twenty at evening parties. Well, it will not be very long before you are of age and free from the restraints of tutelage. So I don't think your guardian's consent is, after all, a matter of any importance.

Jack. Pray excuse me, Lady Bracknell, for interrupting you again, but it is only fair to tell you that according to the terms of her grandfather's will Miss Cardew does not come legally of age till she is thirty-five.

Lady Bracknell. That does not seem to me to be a grave objection. Thirty- five is a very attractive age. London society is full of women of the very highest birth who have, of their own free choice, remained thirty- five for years. Lady Dumbleton is an instance in point. To my own knowledge she has been thirty-five ever since she arrived at the age of forty, which was many years ago now. I see no reason why our dear Cecily should not be even still more attractive at the age you mention than she is at present. There will be a large accumulation of property.

Cecily. Algy, could you wait for me till I was thirty-five?

Algernon. Of course I could, Cecily. You know I could.

Cecily. Yes, I felt it instinctively, but I couldn't wait all that time. I hate waiting even five minutes for anybody. It always makes me rather cross. I am not punctual myself, I know, but I do like punctuality in others, and waiting, even to be married, is quite out of the question.

Algernon. Then what is to be done, Cecily?

Cecily. I don't know, Mr. Moncrieff.

Lady Bracknell. My dear Mr. Worthing, as Miss Cardew states positively that she cannot wait till she is thirty-five--a remark which I am bound to say seems to me to show a somewhat impatient nature--I would beg of you to reconsider your decision.

Jack. But my dear Lady Bracknell, the matter is entirely in your own hands. The moment you consent to my marriage with Gwendolen, I will most gladly allow your nephew to form an alliance with my ward.

Lady Bracknell. [Rising and drawing herself up.] You must be quite aware that what you propose is out of the question.

Jack. Then a passionate celibacy is all that any of us can look forward to.

Lady Bracknell. That is not the destiny I propose for Gwendolen. Algernon, of course, can choose for himself. [Pulls out her watch.] Come, dear, [Gwendolen rises] we have already missed five, if not six, trains. To miss any more might expose us to comment on the platform.

[Enter Dr. Chasuble.]

Chasuble. Everything is quite ready for the christenings.

Lady Bracknell. The christenings, sir! Is not that somewhat premature?

Chasuble. [Looking rather puzzled, and pointing to Jack and Algernon.] Both these gentlemen have expressed a desire for immediate baptism.

Lady Bracknell. At their age? The idea is grotesque and irreligious! Algernon, I forbid you to be baptized. I will not hear of such excesses. Lord Bracknell would be highly displeased if he learned that that was the way in which you wasted your time and money.

Chasuble. Am I to understand then that there are to be no christenings at all this afternoon?

Jack. I don't think that, as things are now, it would be of much practical value to either of us, Dr. Chasuble.

Chasuble. I am grieved to hear such sentiments from you, Mr. Worthing. They savour of the heretical views of the Anabaptists, views that I have completely refuted in four of my unpublished sermons. However, as your present mood seems to be one peculiarly secular, I will return to the church at once. Indeed, I have just been informed by the pew-opener that for the last hour and a half Miss Prism has been waiting for me in the vestry.

Lady Bracknell. [Starting.] Miss Prism! Did I hear you mention a Miss Prism?

Chasuble. Yes, Lady Bracknell. I am on my way to join her.

Lady Bracknell. Pray allow me to detain you for a moment. This matter may prove to be one of vital importance to Lord Bracknell and myself. Is this Miss Prism a female of repellent aspect, remotely connected with education?

Chasuble. [Somewhat indignantly.] She is the most cultivated of ladies, and the very picture of respectability.

Lady Bracknell. It is obviously the same person. May I ask what position she holds in your household?

Chasuble. [Severely.] I am a celibate, madam.

Jack. [Interposing.] Miss Prism, Lady Bracknell, has been for the last three years Miss Cardew's esteemed governess and valued companion.

Lady Bracknell. In spite of what I hear of her, I must see her at once. Let her be sent for.

Chasuble. [Looking off.] She approaches; she is nigh.

[Enter Miss Prism hurriedly.]

Miss Prism. I was told you expected me in the vestry, dear Canon. I have been waiting for you there for an hour and three-quarters. [Catches sight of Lady Bracknell, who has fixed her with a stony glare. Miss Prism grows pale and quails. She looks anxiously round as if desirous to escape.]

Lady Bracknell. [In a severe, judicial voice.] Prism! [Miss Prism bows her head in shame.] Come here, Prism! [Miss Prism approaches in a humble manner.] Prism! Where is that baby? [General consternation. The Canon starts back in horror. Algernon and Jack pretend to be anxious to shield Cecily and Gwendolen from hearing the details of a terrible public scandal.] Twenty-eight years ago, Prism, you left Lord Bracknell's house, Number 104, Upper Grosvenor Street, in charge of a perambulator that contained a baby of the male sex. You never returned. A few weeks later, through the elaborate investigations of the Metropolitan police, the perambulator was discovered at midnight, standing by itself in a remote corner of Bayswater. It contained the manuscript of a three-volume novel of more than usually revolting sentimentality. [Miss Prism starts in involuntary indignation.] But the baby was not there! [Every one looks at Miss Prism.] Prism! Where is that baby? [A pause.]

Miss Prism. Lady Bracknell, I admit with shame that I do not know. I only wish I did. The plain facts of the case are these. On the morning of the day you mention, a day that is for ever branded on my memory, I prepared as usual to take the baby out in its perambulator. I had also with me a somewhat old, but capacious hand-bag in which I had intended to place the manuscript of a work of fiction that I had written during my few unoccupied hours. In a moment of mental abstraction, for which I never can forgive myself, I deposited the manuscript in the basinette, and placed the baby in the hand-bag.

Jack. [Who has been listening attentively.] But where did you deposit the hand-bag?

Miss Prism. Do not ask me, Mr. Worthing.

Jack. Miss Prism, this is a matter of no small importance to me. I insist on knowing where you deposited the hand-bag that contained that infant.

Miss Prism. I left it in the cloak-room of one of the larger railway stations in London.

Jack. What railway station?

Miss Prism. [Quite crushed.] Victoria. The Brighton line. [Sinks into a chair.]

Jack. I must retire to my room for a moment. Gwendolen, wait here for me.

Gwendolen. If you are not too long, I will wait here for you all my life. [Exit Jack in great excitement.]

Chasuble. What do you think this means, Lady Bracknell?

Lady Bracknell. I dare not even suspect, Dr. Chasuble. I need hardly tell you that in families of high position strange coincidences are not supposed to occur. They are hardly considered the thing.

[Noises heard overhead as if some one was throwing trunks about. Every one looks up.]

Cecily. Uncle Jack seems strangely agitated.

Chasuble. Your guardian has a very emotional nature.

Lady Bracknell. This noise is extremely unpleasant. It sounds as if he was having an argument. I dislike arguments of any kind. They are always vulgar, and often convincing.

Chasuble. [Looking up.] It has stopped now. [The noise is redoubled.]

Lady Bracknell. I wish he would arrive at some conclusion.

Gwendolen. This suspense is terrible. I hope it will last. [Enter Jack with a hand-bag of black leather in his hand.]

Jack. [Rushing over to Miss Prism.] Is this the hand-bag, Miss Prism? Examine it carefully before you speak. The happiness of more than one life depends on your answer.

Miss Prism. [Calmly.] It seems to be mine. Yes, here is the injury it received through the upsetting of a Gower Street omnibus in younger and happier days. Here is the stain on the lining caused by the explosion of a temperance beverage, an incident that occurred at Leamington. And here, on the lock, are my initials. I had forgotten that in an extravagant mood I had had them placed there. The bag is undoubtedly mine. I am delighted to have it so unexpectedly restored to me. It has been a great inconvenience being without it all these years.

Jack. [In a pathetic voice.] Miss Prism, more is restored to you than this hand-bag. I was the baby you placed in it.

Miss Prism. [Amazed.] You?

Jack. [Embracing her.] Yes . . . mother!

Miss Prism. [Recoiling in indignant astonishment.] Mr. Worthing! I am unmarried!

Jack. Unmarried! I do not deny that is a serious blow. But after all, who has the right to cast a stone against one who has suffered? Cannot repentance wipe out an act of folly? Why should there be one law for men, and another for women? Mother, I forgive you. [Tries to embrace her again.]

Miss Prism. [Still more indignant.] Mr. Worthing, there is some error. [Pointing to Lady Bracknell.] There is the lady who can tell you who you really are.

Jack. [After a pause.] Lady Bracknell, I hate to seem inquisitive, but would you kindly inform me who I am?

Lady Bracknell. I am afraid that the news I have to give you will not altogether please you. You are the son of my poor sister, Mrs. Moncrieff, and consequently Algernon's elder brother.

Jack. Algy's elder brother! Then I have a brother after all. I knew I had a brother! I always said I had a brother! Cecily,--how could you have ever doubted that I had a brother? [Seizes hold of Algernon.] Dr. Chasuble, my unfortunate brother. Miss Prism, my unfortunate brother. Gwendolen, my unfortunate brother. Algy, you young scoundrel, you will have to treat me with more respect in the future. You have never behaved to me like a brother in all your life.

Algernon. Well, not till to-day, old boy, I admit. I did my best, however, though I was out of practice.

[Shakes hands.]

Gwendolen. [To Jack.] My own! But what own are you? What is your Christian name, now that you have become some one else?

Jack. Good heavens! . . . I had quite forgotten that point. Your decision on the subject of my name is irrevocable, I suppose?

Gwendolen. I never change, except in my affections.

Cecily. What a noble nature you have, Gwendolen!

Jack. Then the question had better be cleared up at once. Aunt Augusta, a moment. At the time when Miss Prism left me in the hand-bag, had I been christened already?

Lady Bracknell. Every luxury that money could buy, including christening, had been lavished on you by your fond and doting parents.

Jack. Then I was christened! That is settled. Now, what name was I given? Let me know the worst.

Lady Bracknell. Being the eldest son you were naturally christened after your father.

Jack. [Irritably.] Yes, but what was my father's Christian name?

Lady Bracknell. [Meditatively.] I cannot at the present moment recall what the General's Christian name was. But I have no doubt he had one. He was eccentric, I admit. But only in later years. And that was the result of the Indian climate, and marriage, and indigestion, and other things of that kind.

Jack. Algy! Can't you recollect what our father's Christian name was?

Algernon. My dear boy, we were never even on speaking terms. He died before I was a year old.

Jack. His name would appear in the Army Lists of the period, I suppose, Aunt Augusta?

Lady Bracknell. The General was essentially a man of peace, except in his domestic life. But I have no doubt his name would appear in any military directory.

Jack. The Army Lists of the last forty years are here. These delightful records should have been my constant study. [Rushes to bookcase and tears the books out.] M. Generals . . . Mallam, Maxbohm, Magley, what ghastly names they have--Markby, Migsby, Mobbs, Moncrieff! Lieutenant 1840, Captain, Lieutenant-Colonel, Colonel, General 1869, Christian names, Ernest John. [Puts book very quietly down and speaks quite calmly.] I always told you, Gwendolen, my name was Ernest, didn't I? Well, it is Ernest after all. I mean it naturally is Ernest.

Lady Bracknell. Yes, I remember now that the General was called Ernest, I knew I had some particular reason for disliking the name.

Gwendolen. Ernest! My own Ernest! I felt from the first that you could have no other name!

Jack. Gwendolen, it is a terrible thing for a man to find out suddenly that all his life he has been speaking nothing but the truth. Can you forgive me?

Gwendolen. I can. For I feel that you are sure to change.

Jack. My own one!

Chasuble. [To Miss Prism.] Laetitia! [Embraces her]

Miss Prism. [Enthusiastically.] Frederick! At last!

Algernon. Cecily! [Embraces her.] At last!

Jack. Gwendolen! [Embraces her.] At last!

Lady Bracknell. My nephew, you seem to be displaying signs of triviality.

Jack. On the contrary, Aunt Augusta, I've now realised for the first time in my life the vital Importance of Being Earnest.

About BookCaps

We all need refreshers every now and then. Whether you are a student trying to cram for that big final, or someone just trying to understand a book more, BookCaps can help. We are a small, but growing company, and are adding titles every month.

Visit www.bookcaps.com to see more of our books, or contact us with any questions.

Made in the USA
Lexington, KY
19 July 2013